1001 Drum Grooves

The Complete Resource for Every Drummer

by Steve Mansfield

ISBN 978-1-57560-419-0

Visit our website at www.cherrylane.com

HOW TO USE THIS BOOK

This book is a collection of grooves from various styles of music and provides an introduction to styles of music you may not be familiar with. I recommend that you listen to the styles of music featured in this book. The importance of listening cannot be stressed enough.

The first section of this book deals with rock, funk, blues, 12/8, and shuffles. At the end of each of these sections, there is a section entitled "Applications." The "Applications" sections are to be used with the material preceding it. You should apply each of the applications to the bass drum part of each of the grooves. This will give you an enormous wealth of different feels for each one. In addition, I encourage you to come up with your own original applications to these grooves. Also, you can mix and match a bar of each of the grooves together to create even more grooves for you to play and work on.

There are lots of great books available encompassing a wide range of drumming styles, so search them out and continue growing. Look at every new thing you learn as a building block that strengthens that which you already know. Oh yeah, and have fun!

ABOUT THE AUTHOR

Steve Mansfield has been working as a professional musician since 1990. He has performed all over the northeastern United States and especially in the New York City area. Steve has performed at jazz and music festivals and has toured Europe. His playing encompasses a wide range of musical styles, including funk, rock, folk, blues, Afro-Cuban, Caribbean, big band, small group jazz, and world music.

Steve's educational background includes a Bachelor of Music degree in Jazz Performance from New York University as well as personal instruction from some of the best instructors in the tri-state area, including John Riley, Adam Nussbaum, Kim Plainfield, Frankie Malabe, Warren Odze, Arthur Lipner, Pete Abbott, Jim Mola, Sherie Miracle, Bill Cerulli, and bassist Mike Richmond.

Steve has been teaching drum set since 1988. His students have received college scholarships, won regional competitions, and ranked high in national competitions. Currently, he is teaching privately, at stores, and at conservatories in New York and Connecticut. He performs regularly with different groups and freelances in the New York metro area.

Steve currently resides in Westchester County, New York.

CONTENTS

Rock (straight eighth)

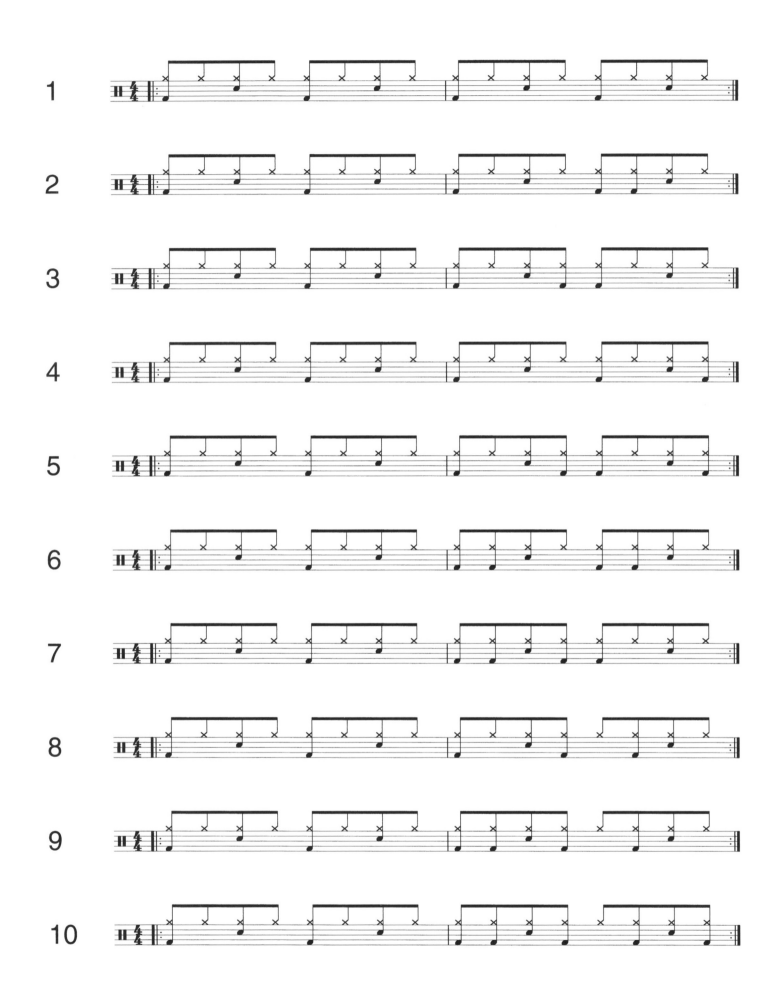

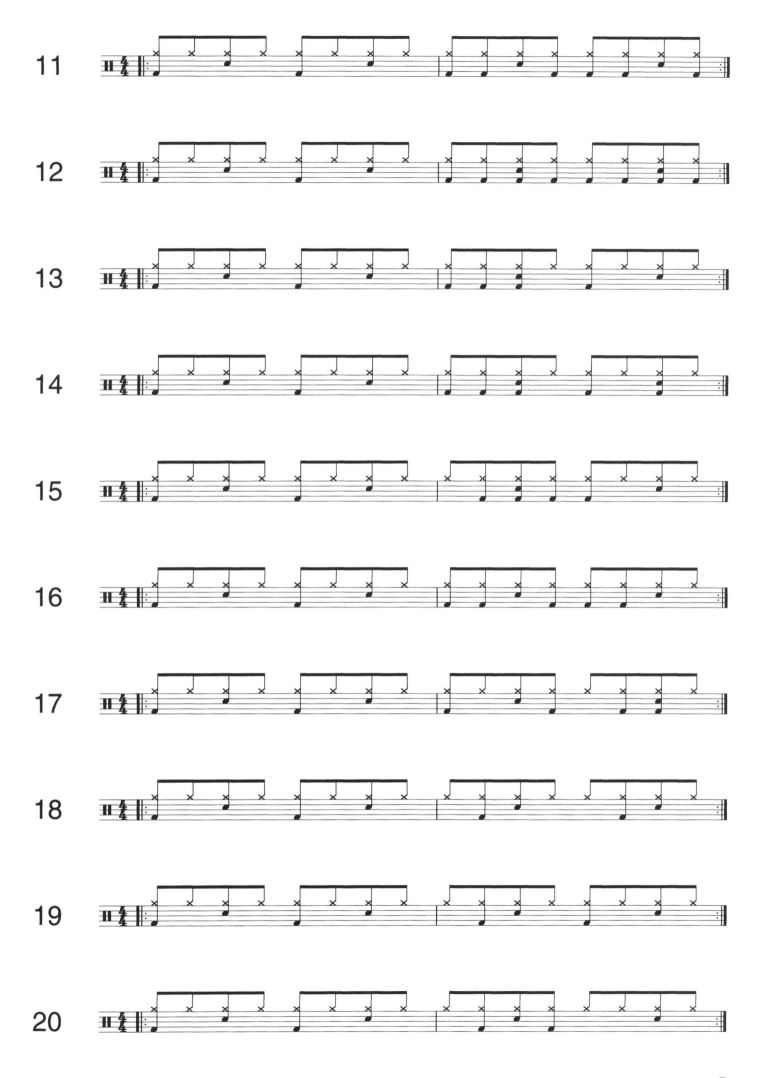

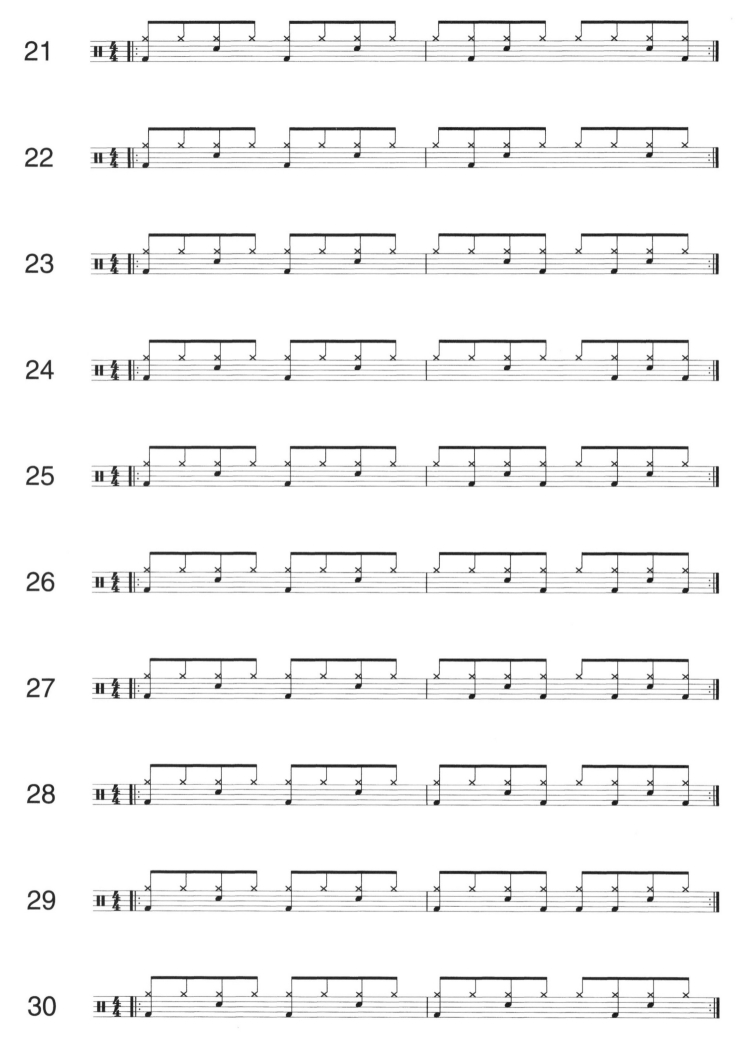

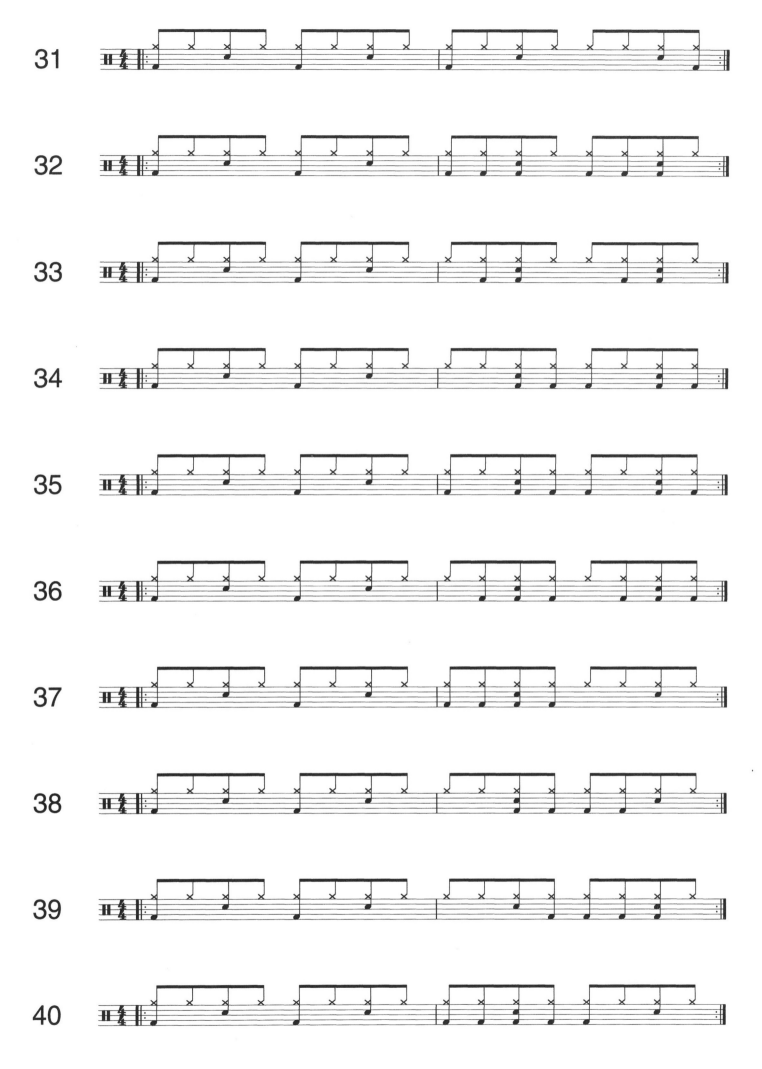

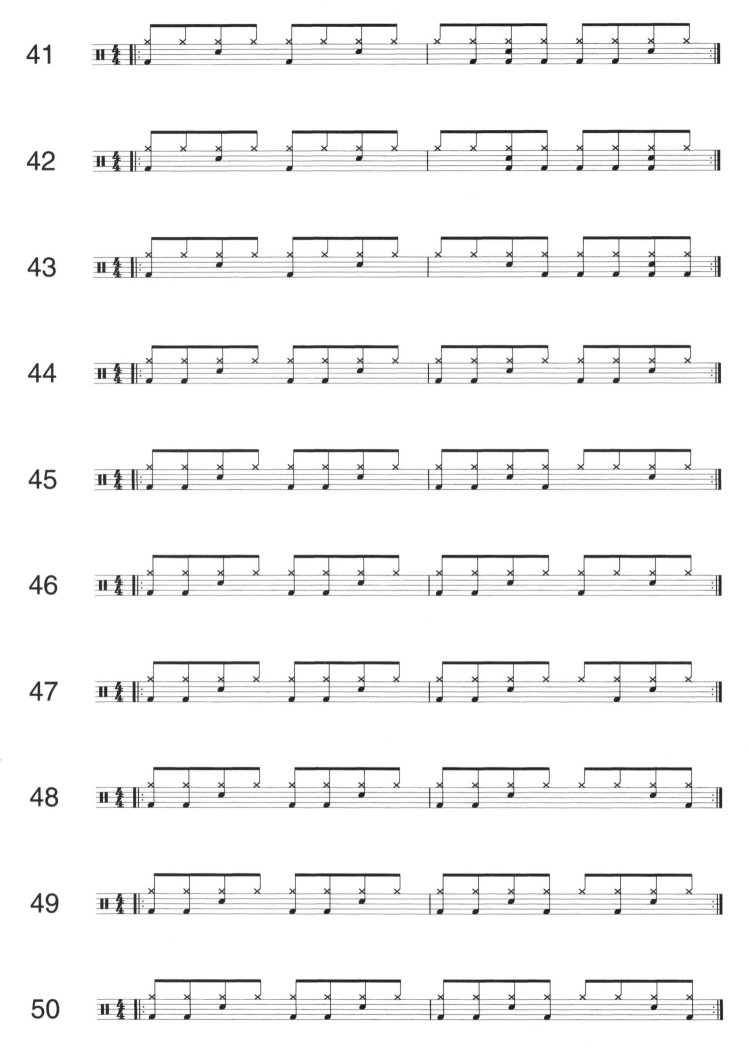

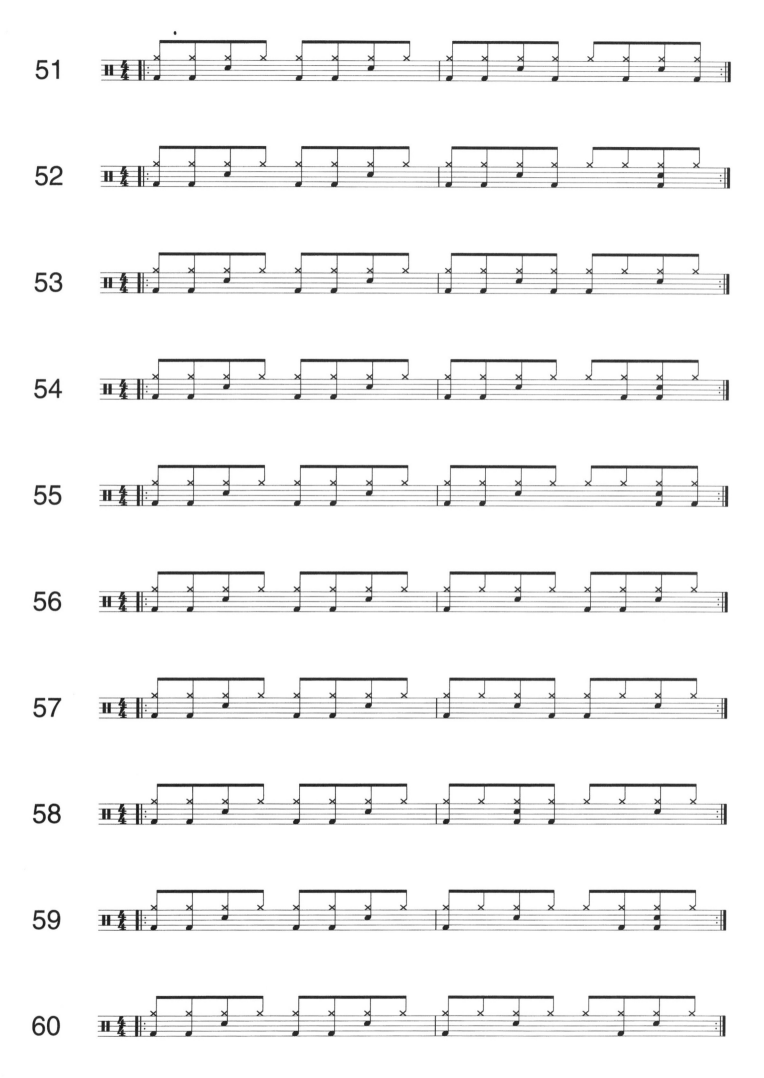

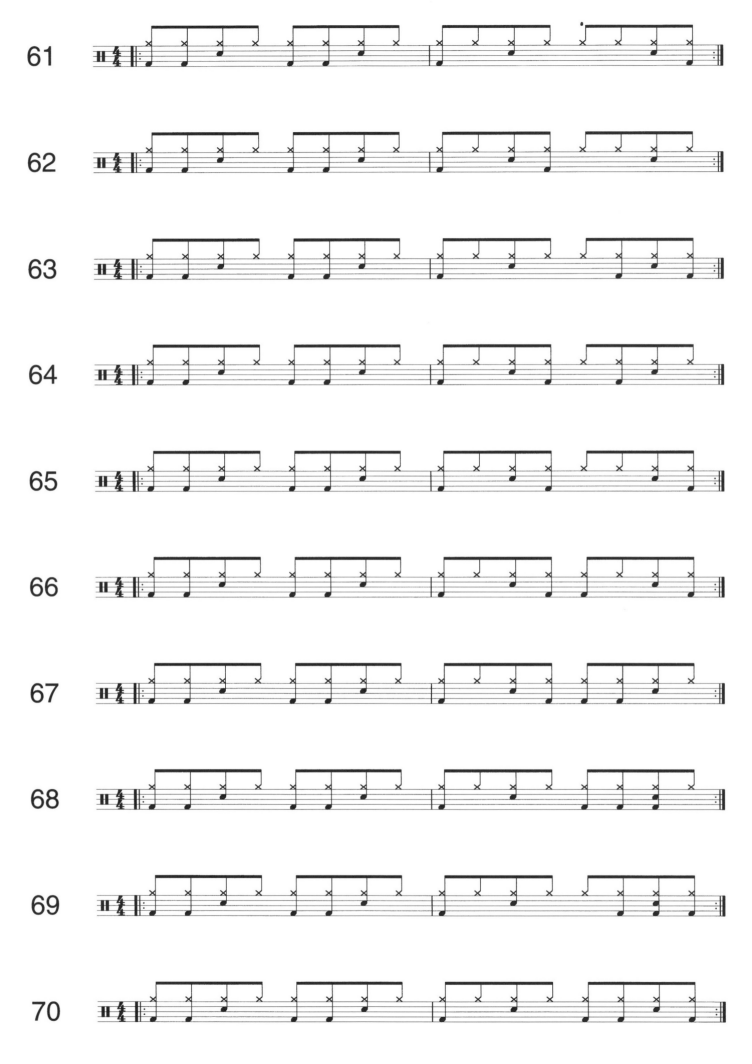

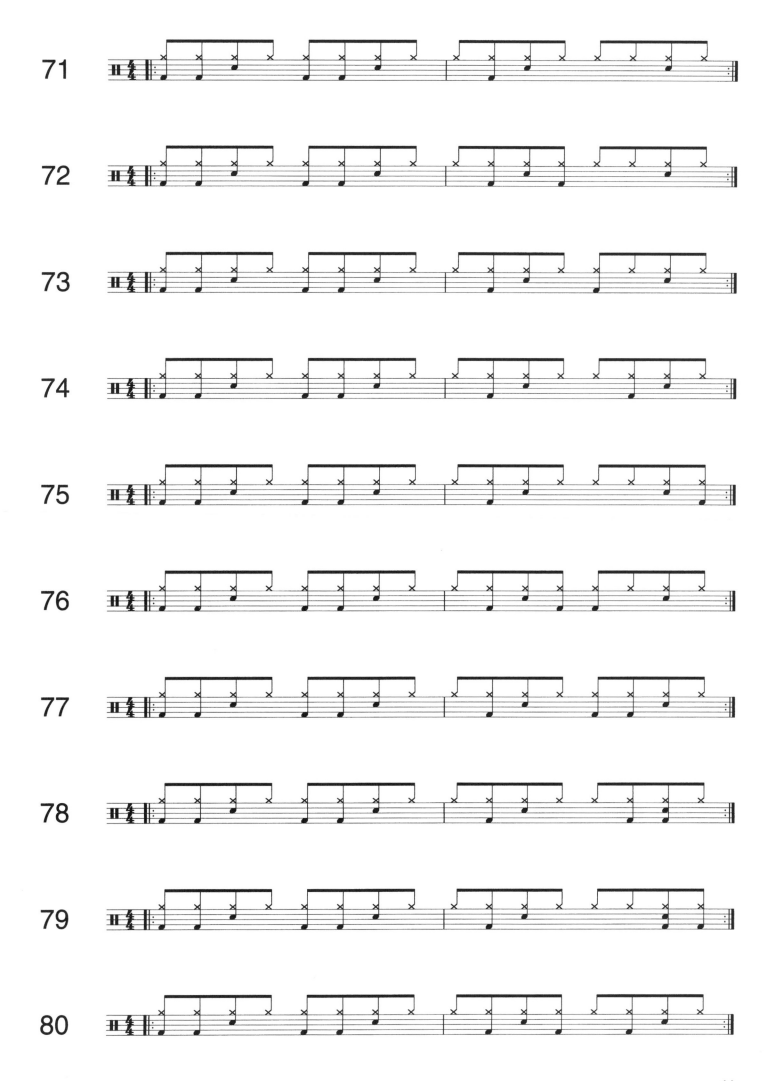

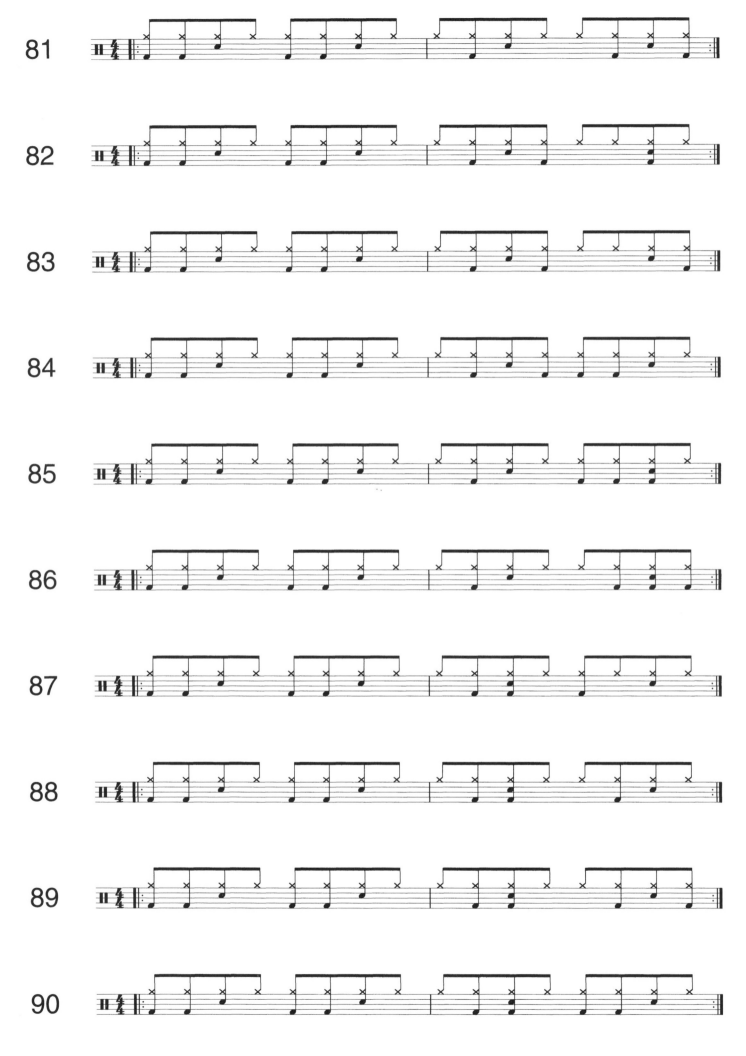

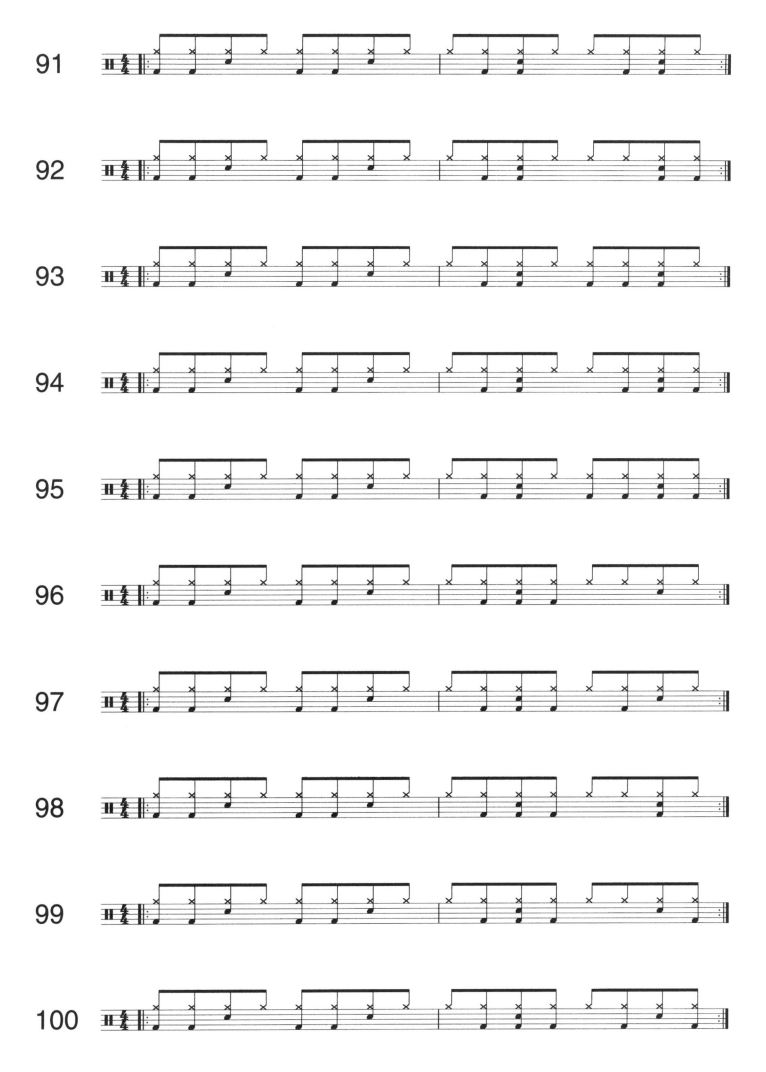

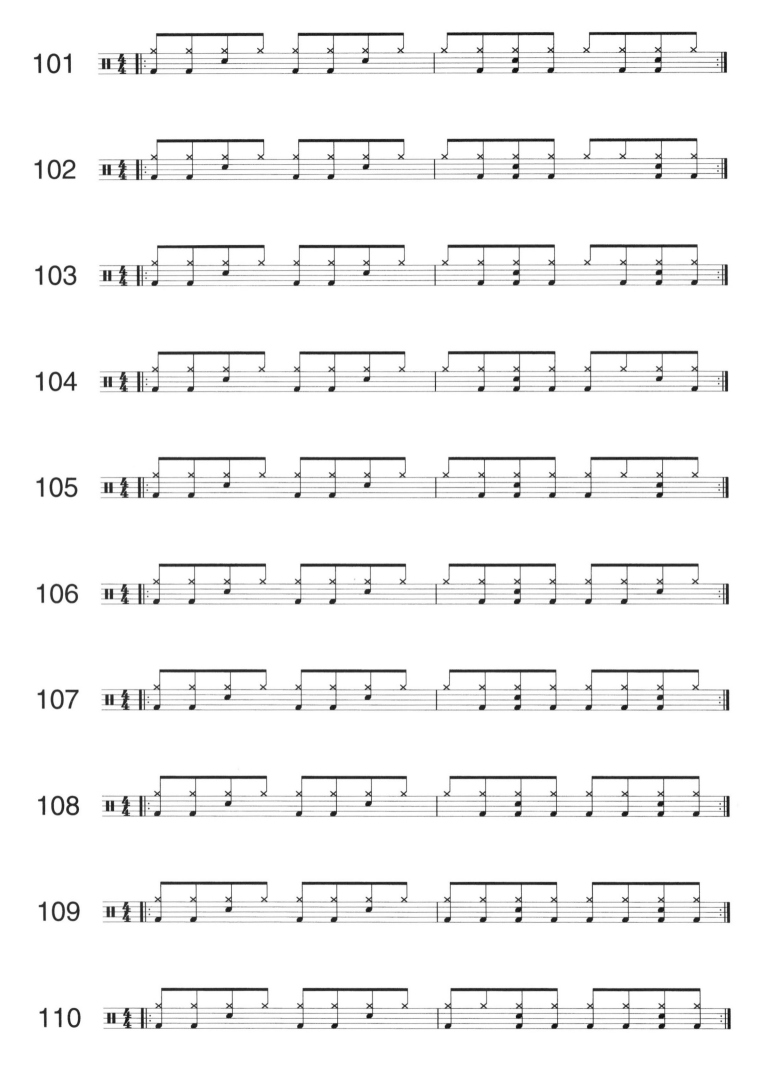

14

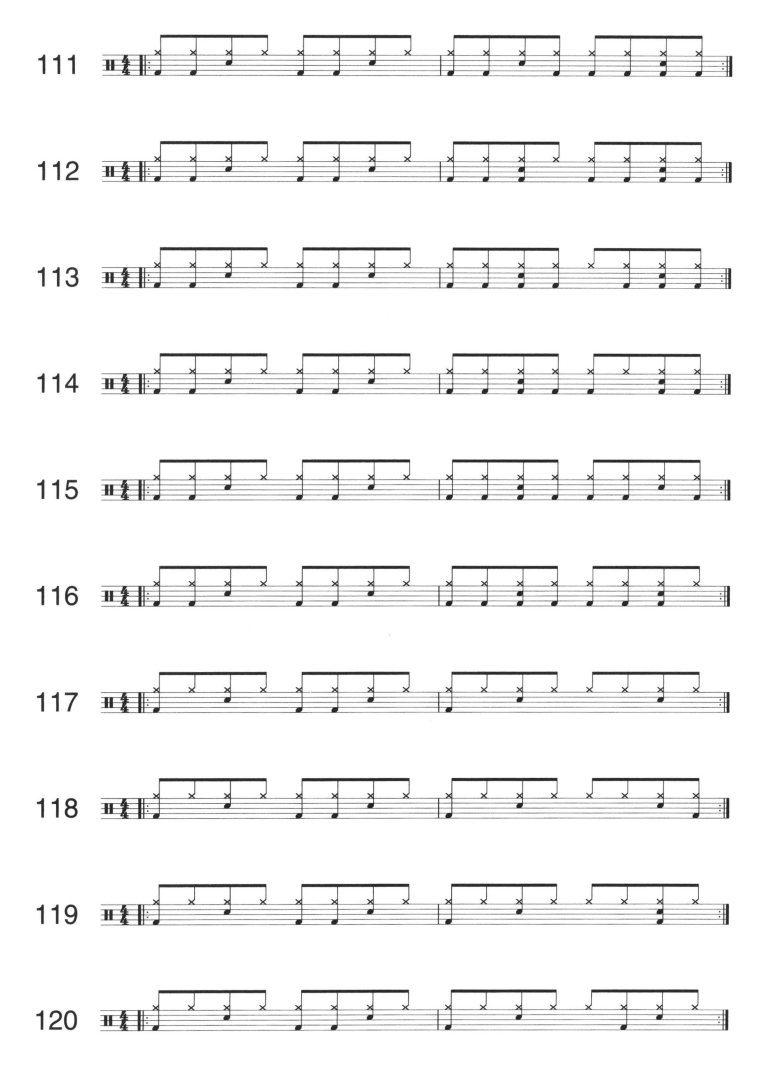

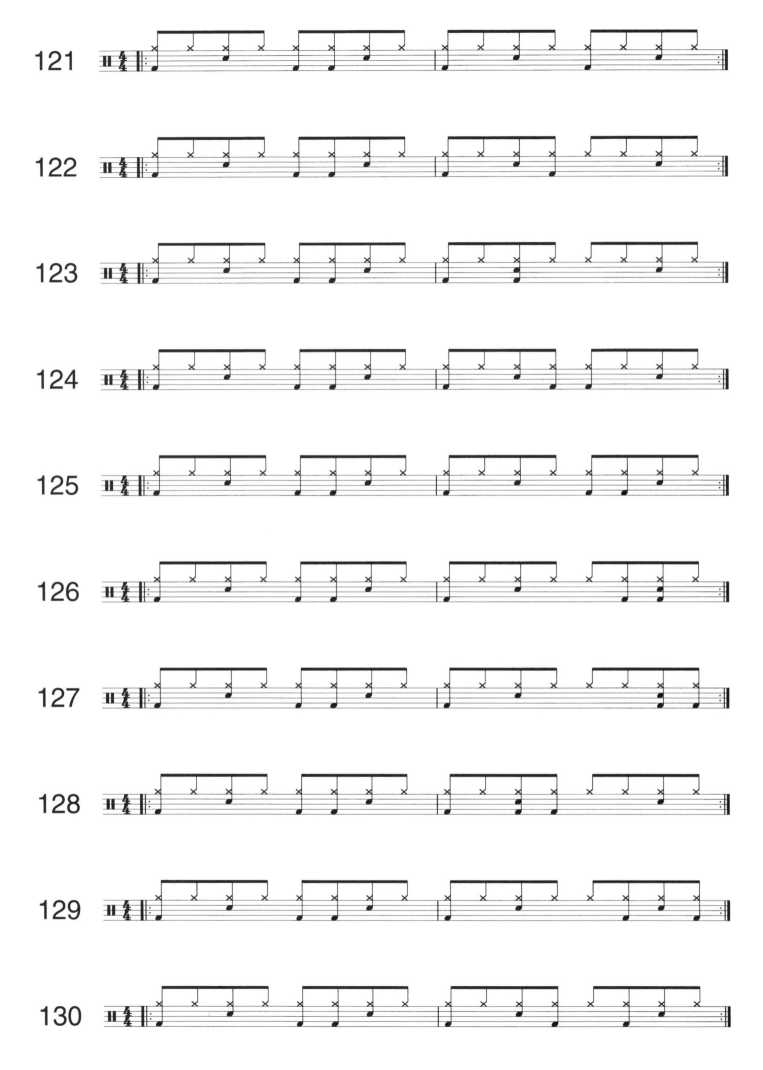

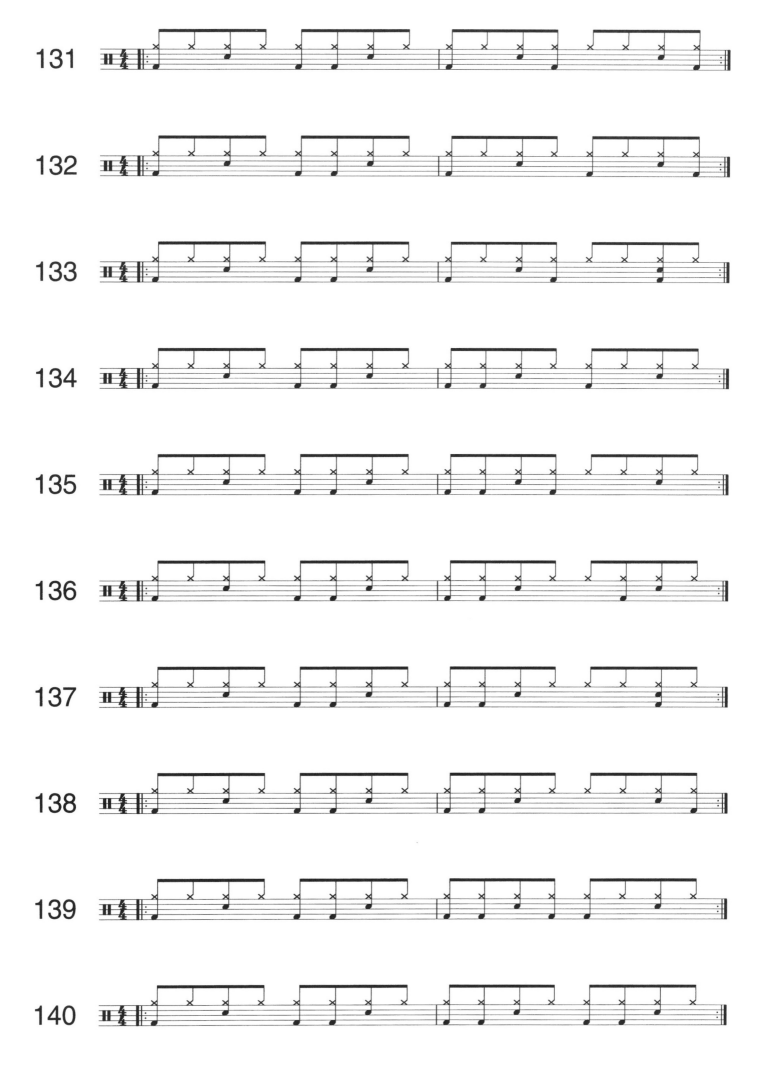

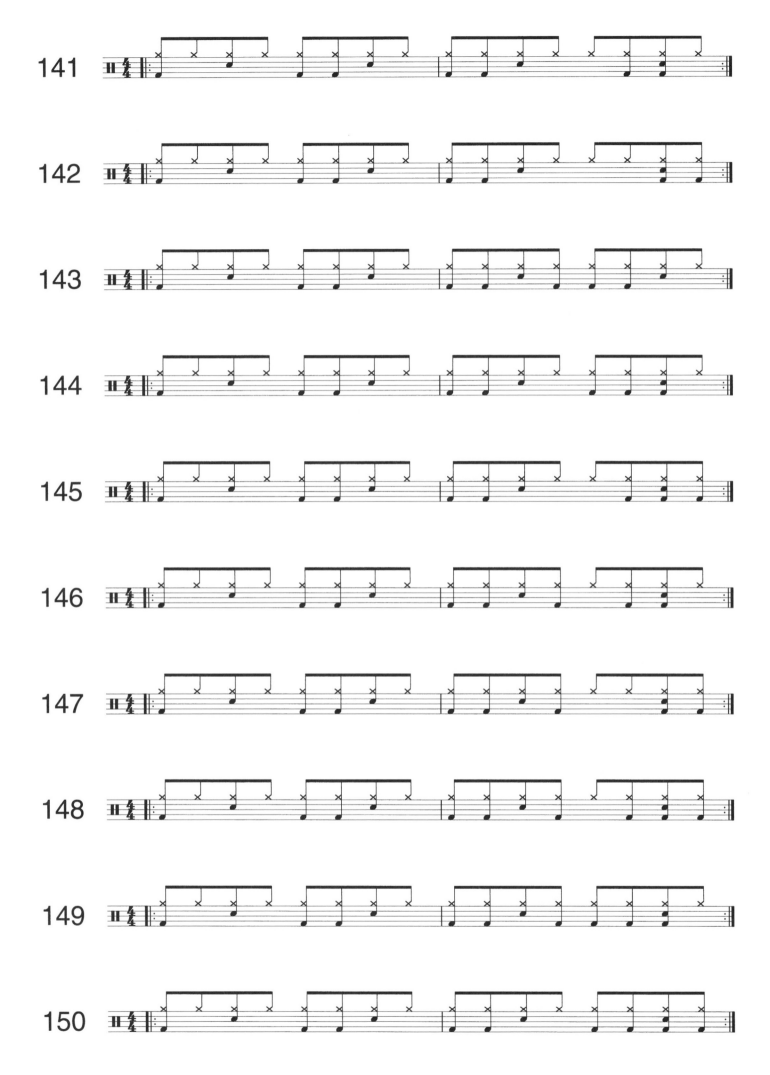

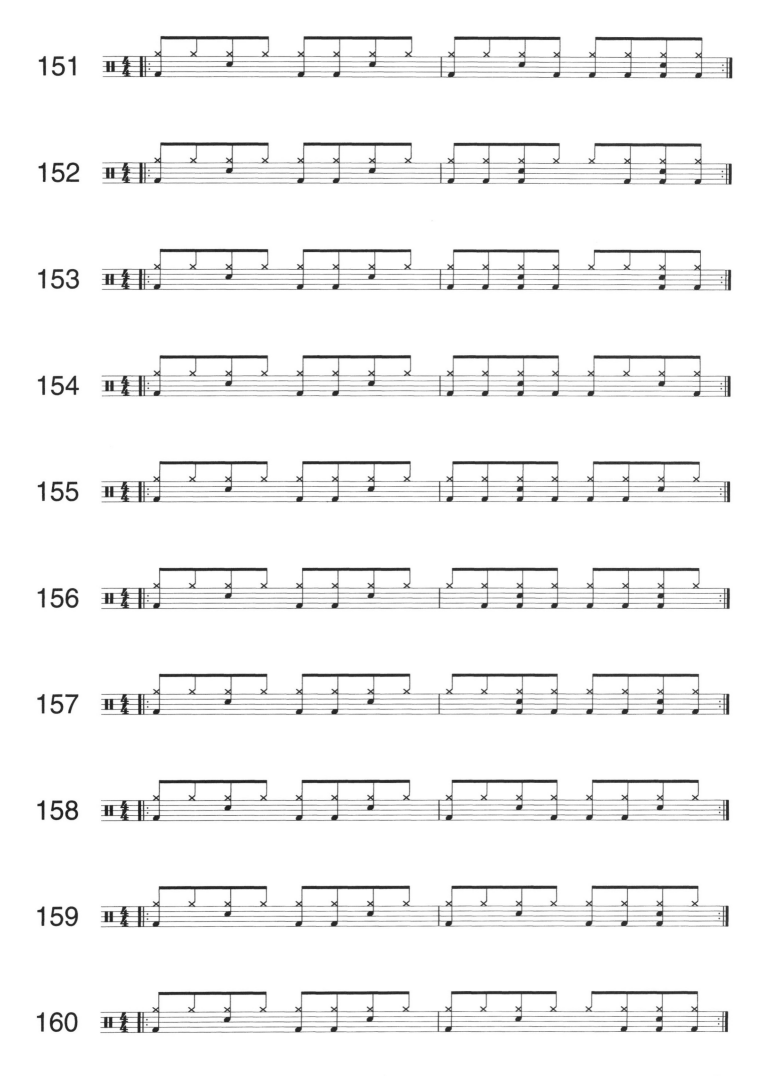

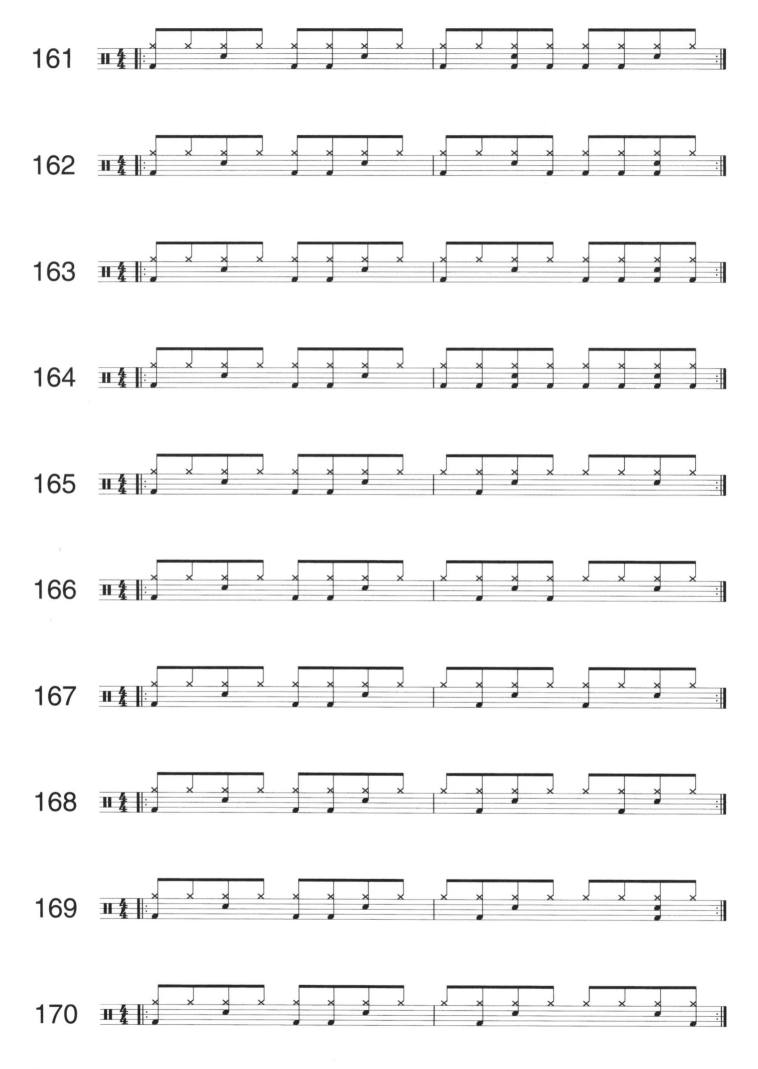

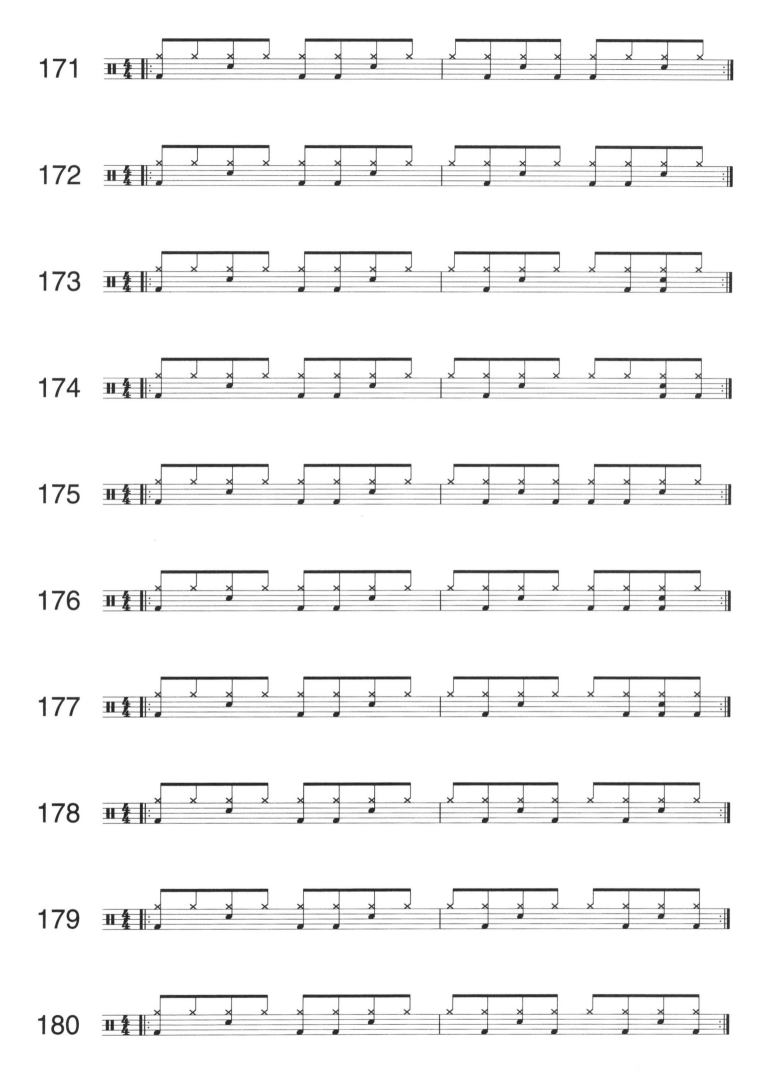

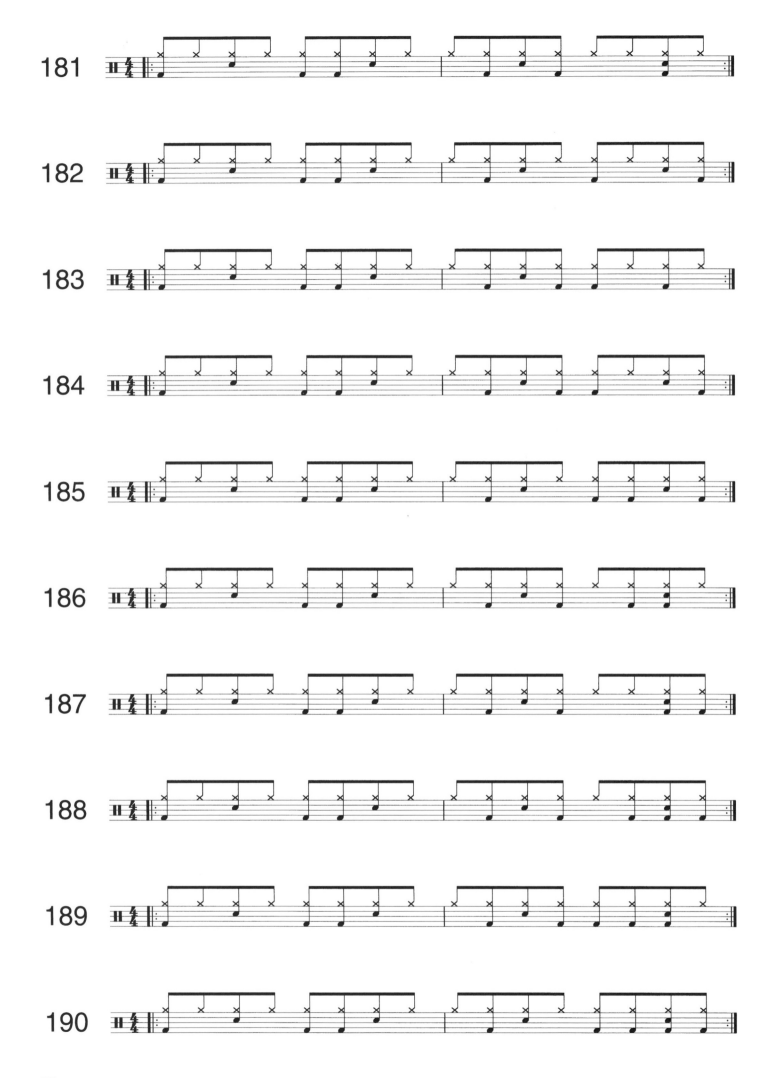

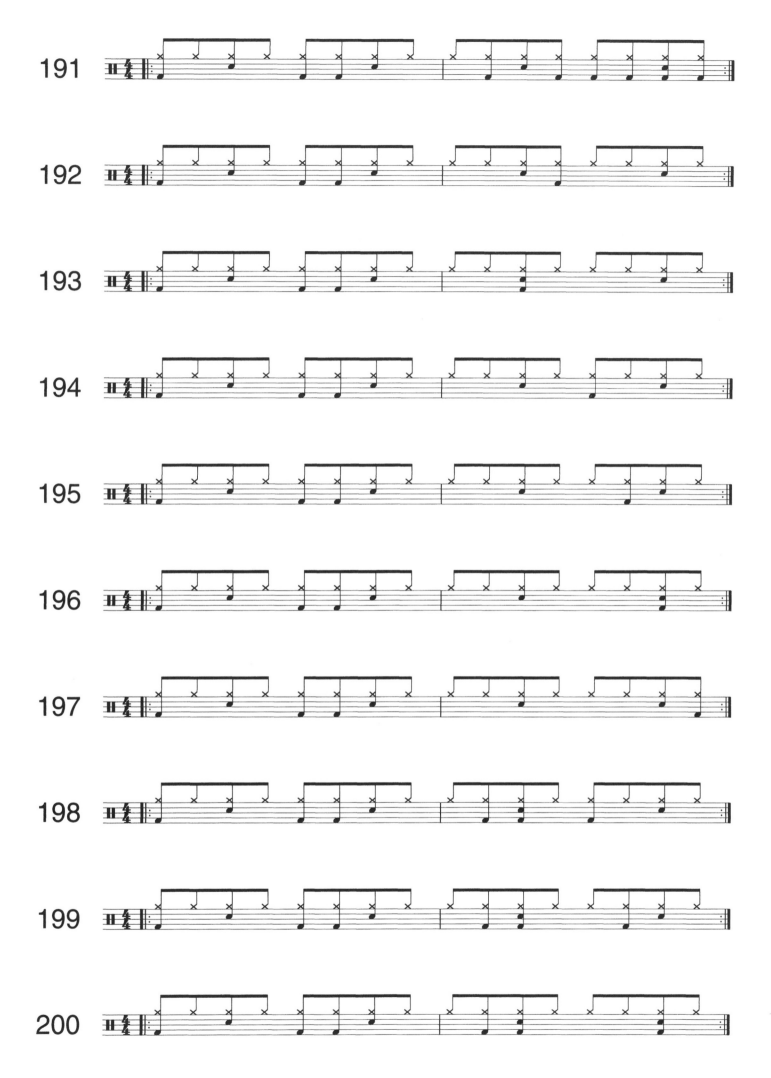

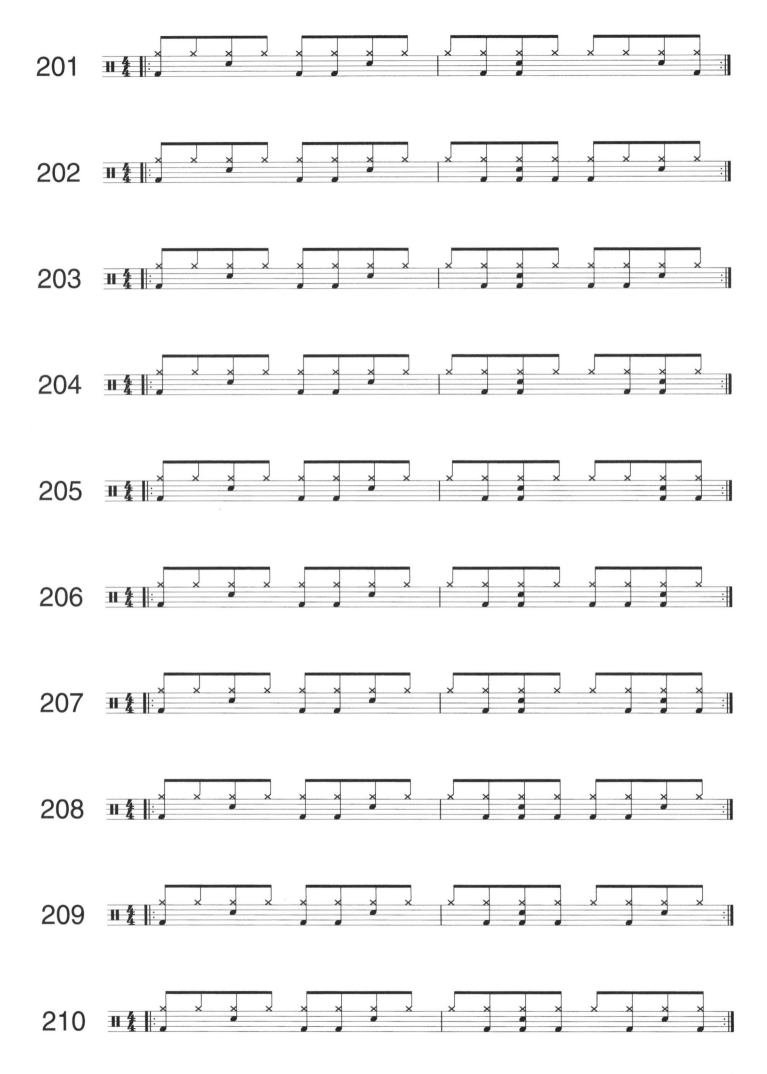

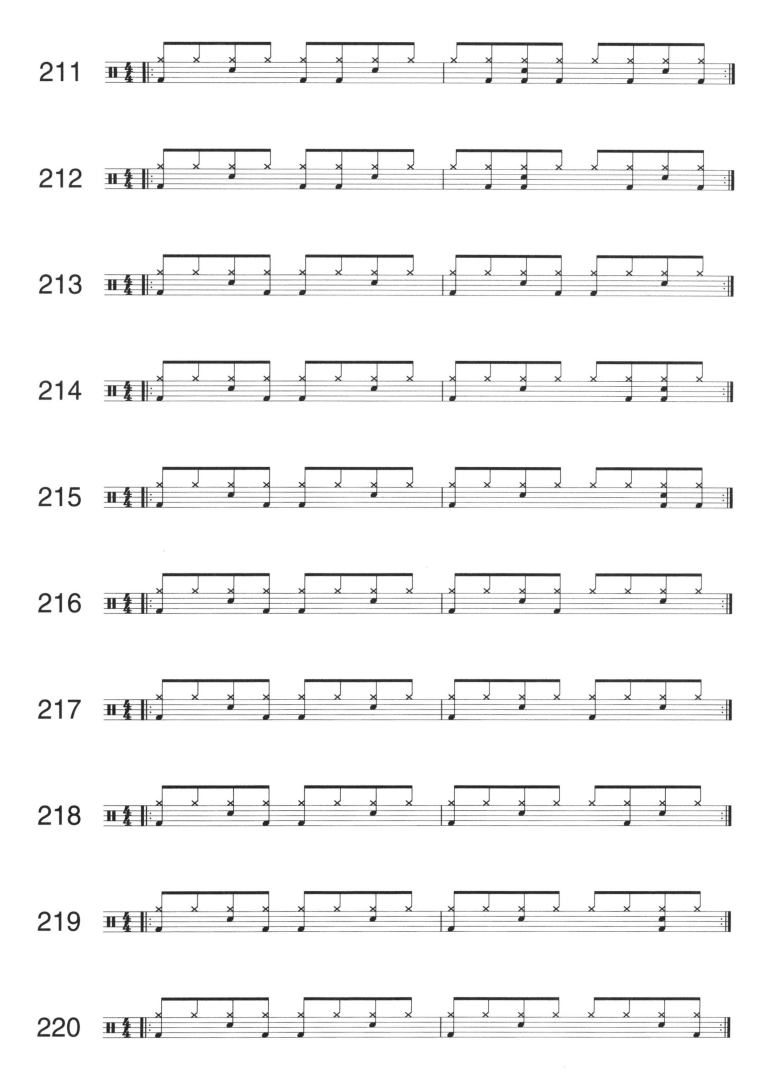

211

212

213

214

215

216

217

218

219

220

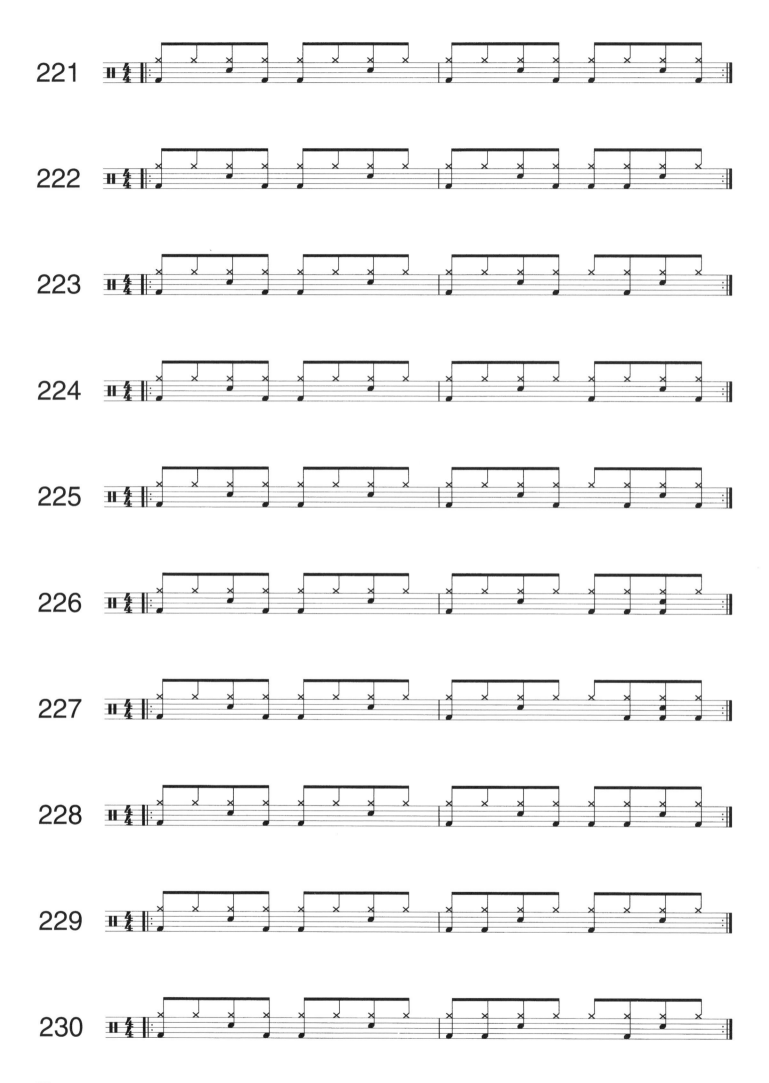

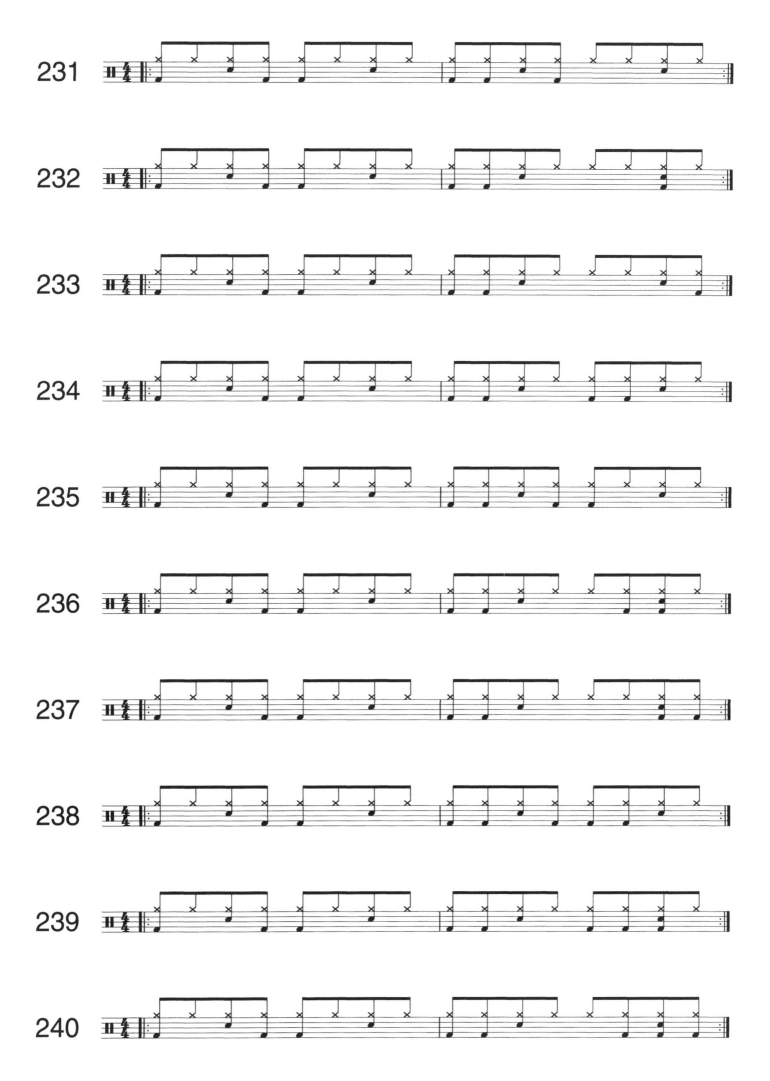

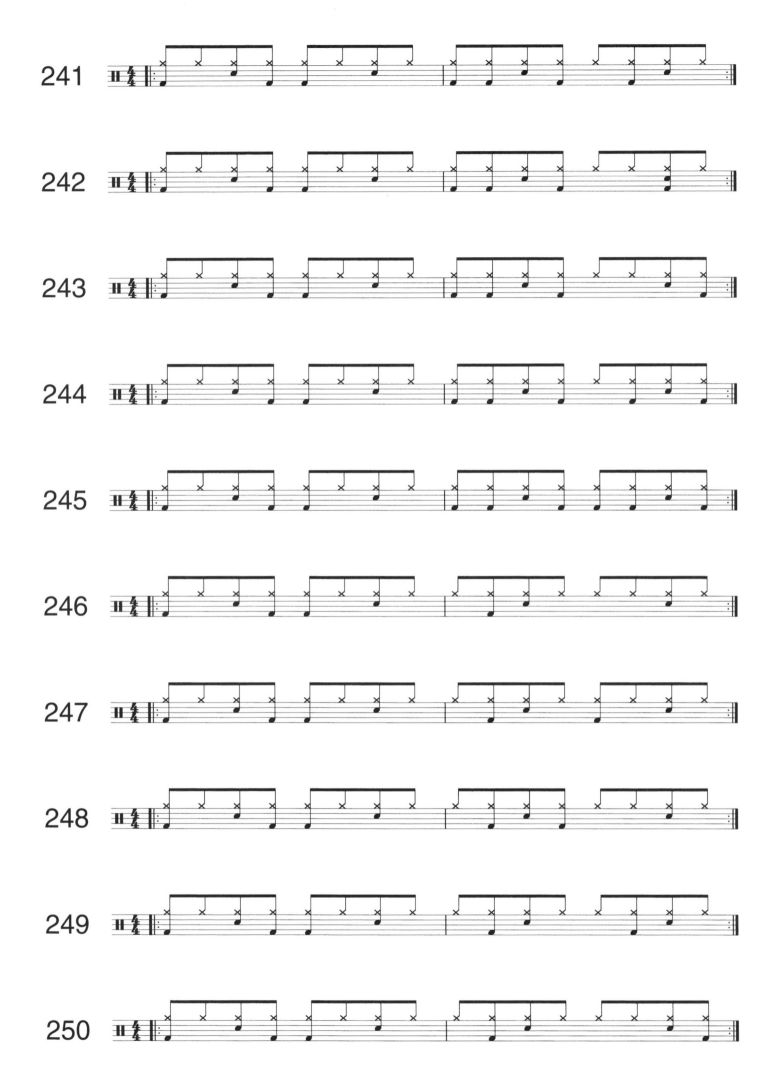

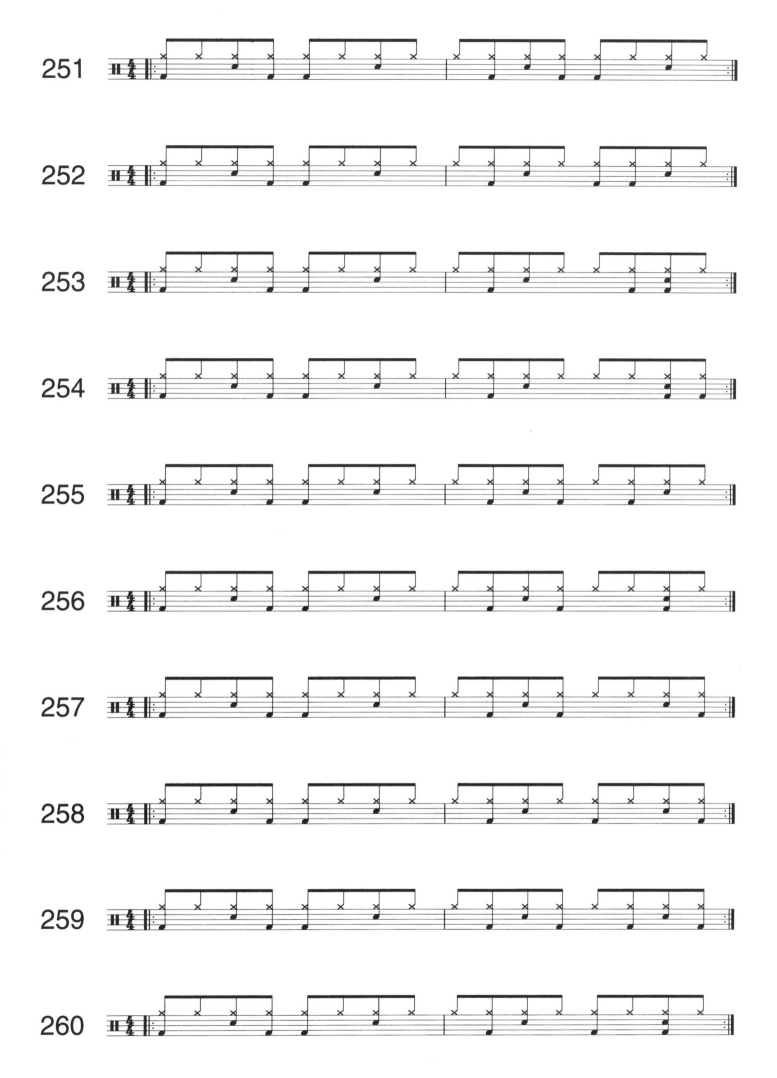

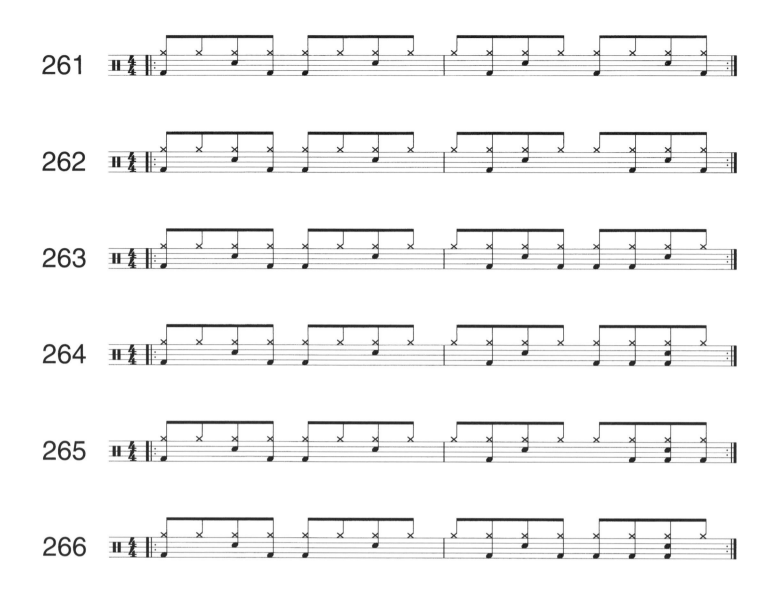

Funk/Rock (sixteenth notes)

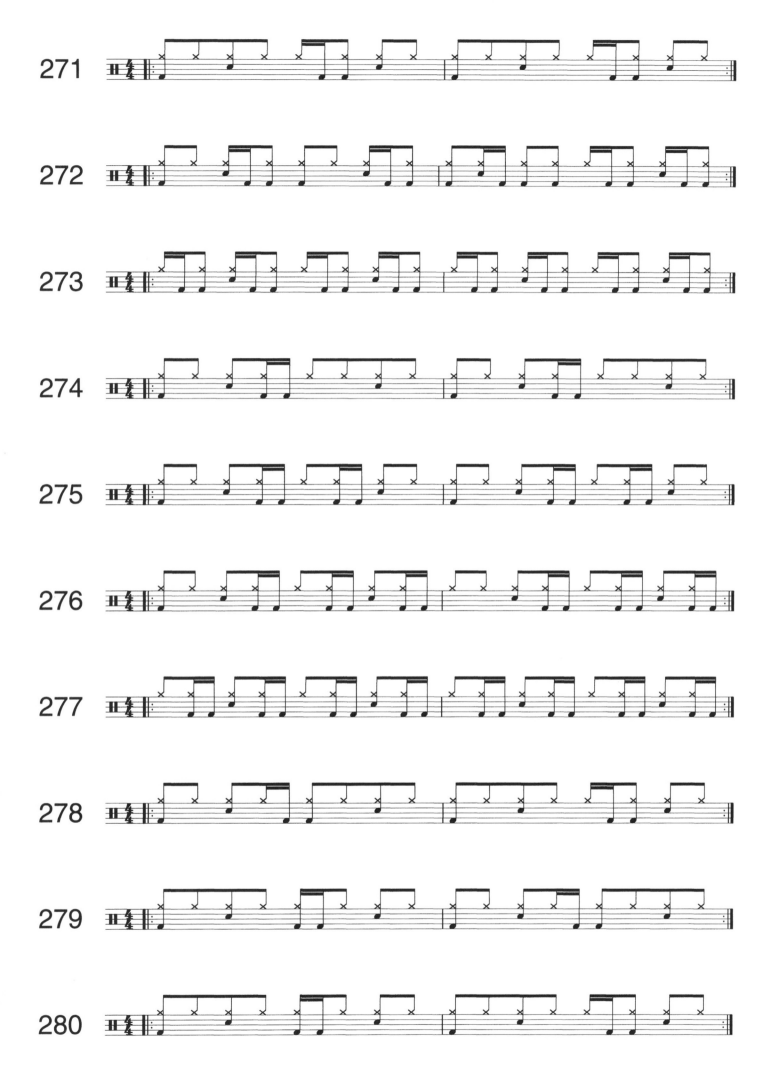

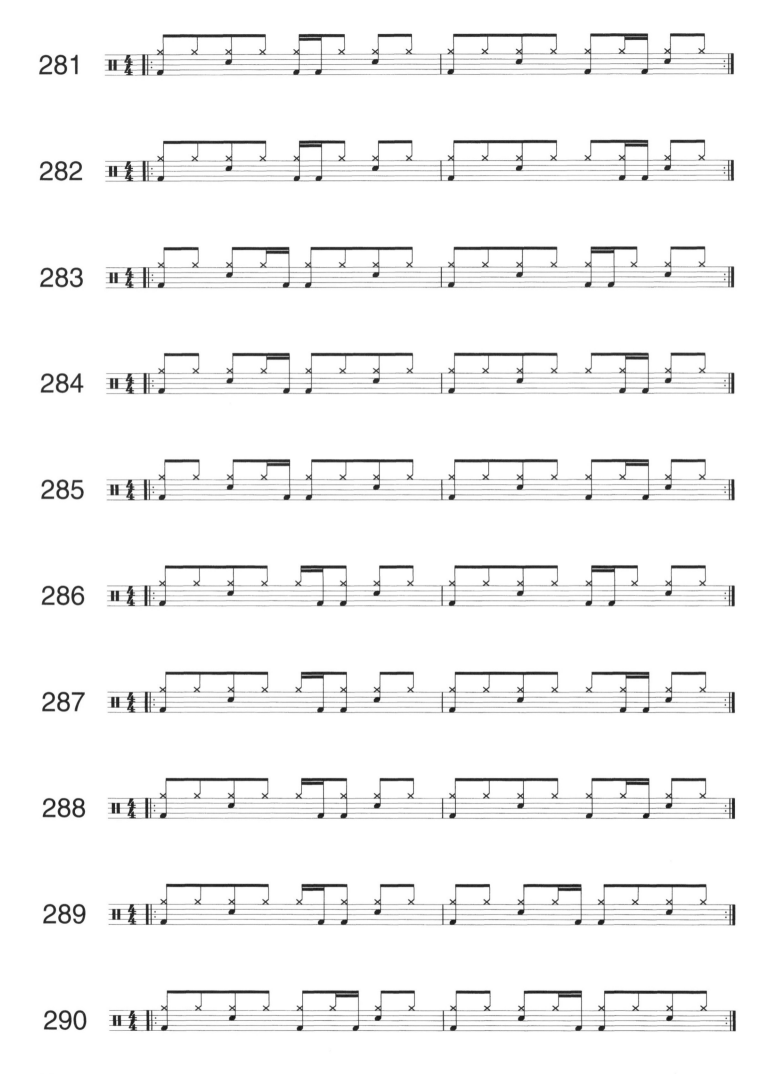

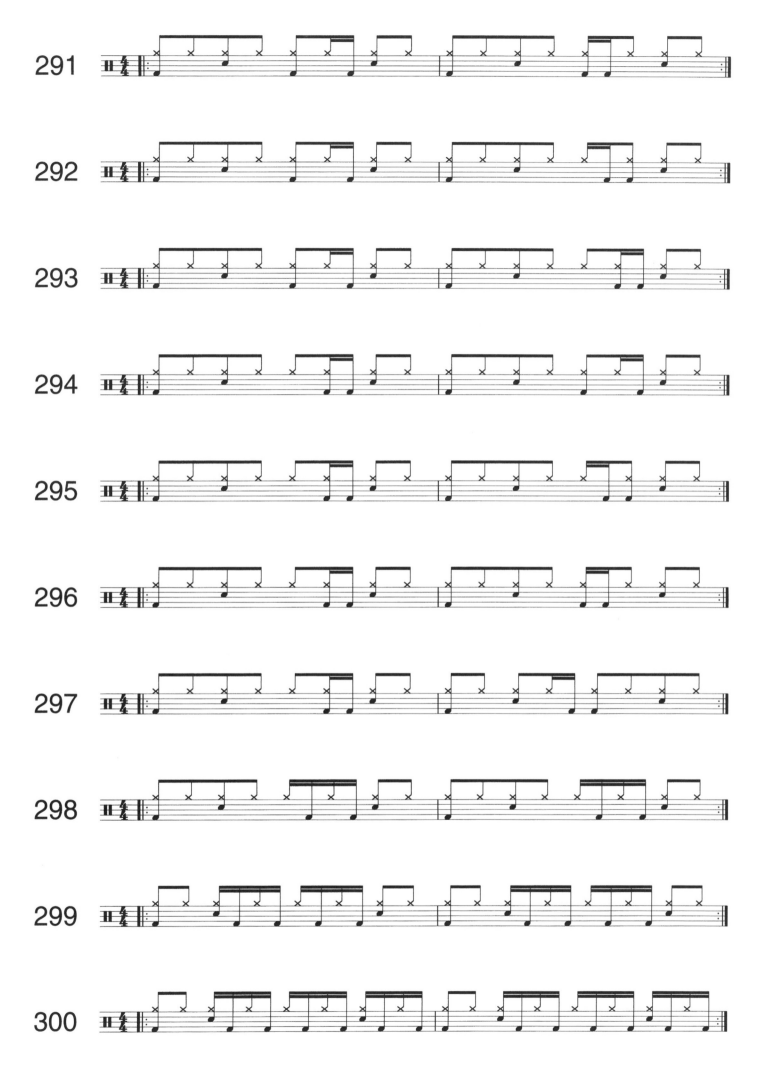

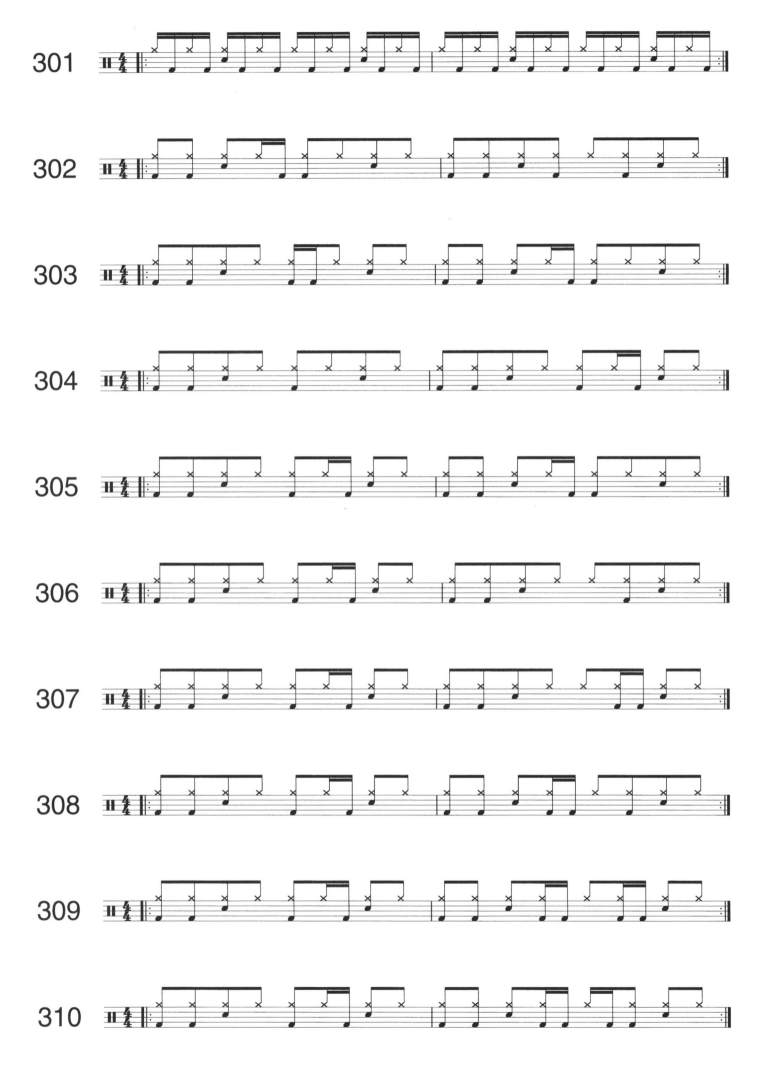

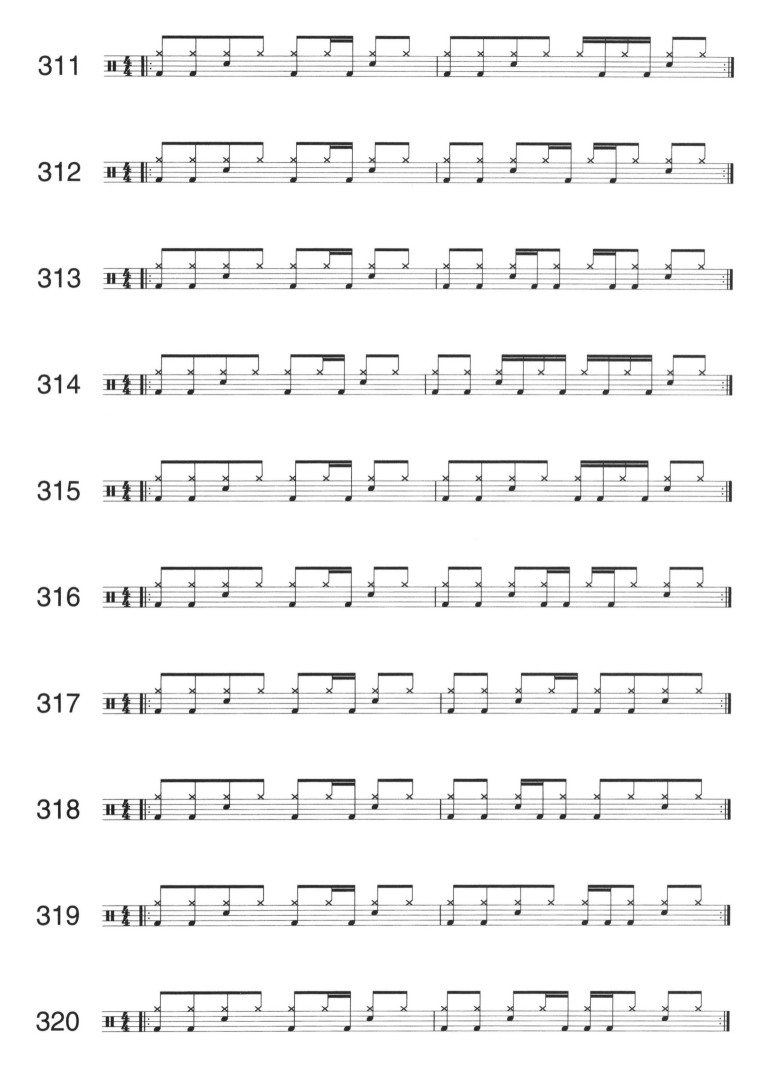

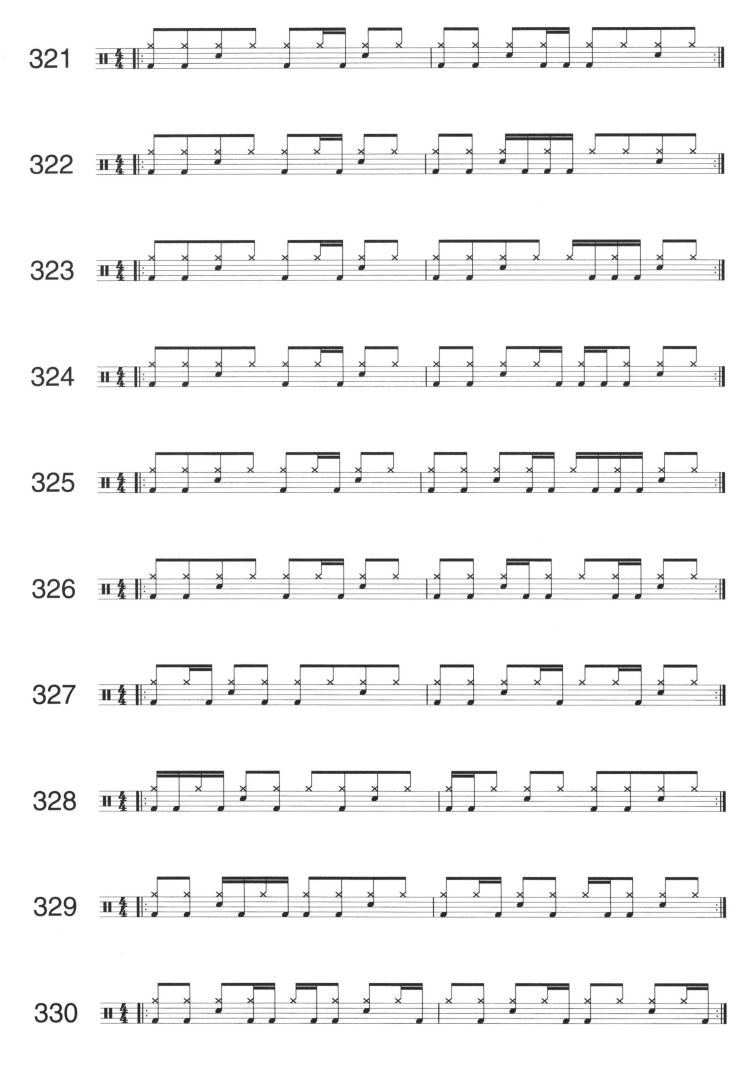

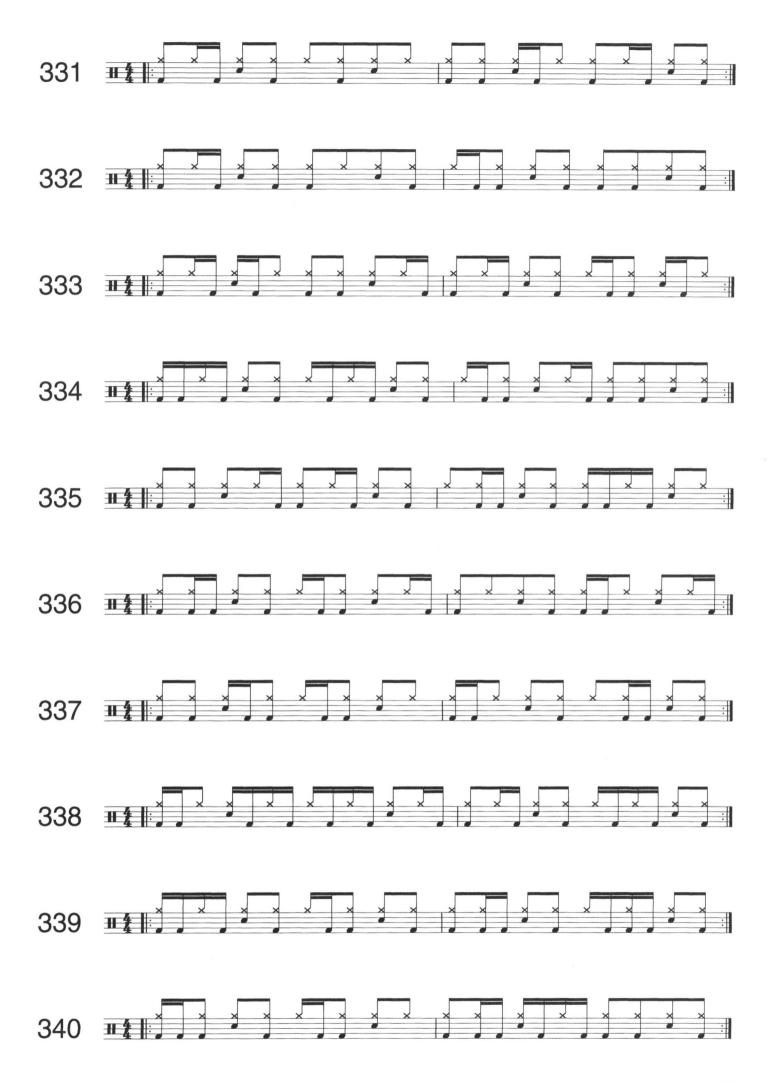

Applications

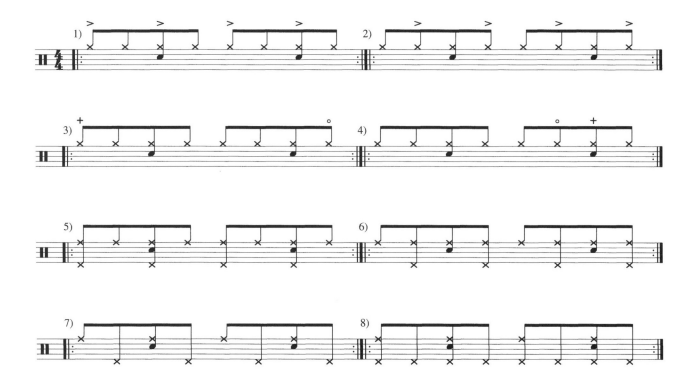

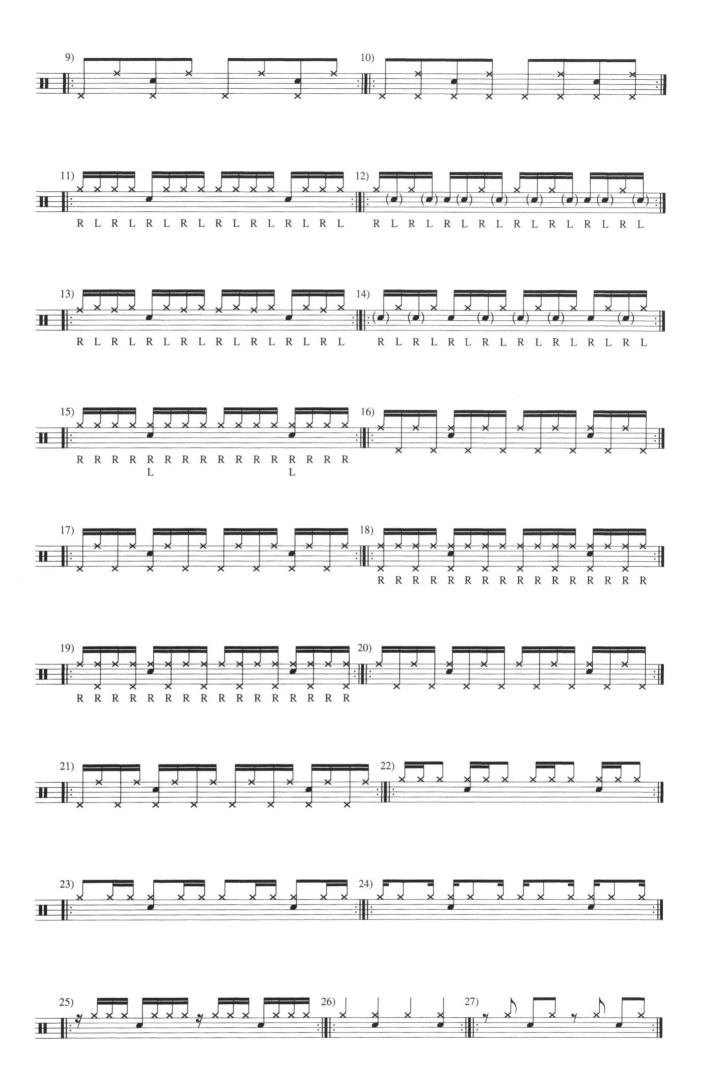

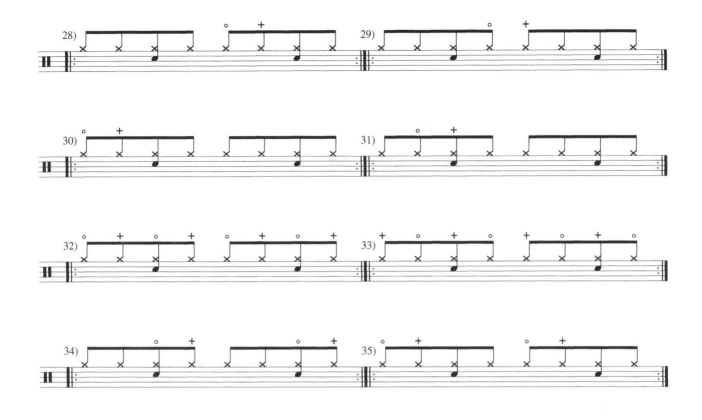

Funk Grooves

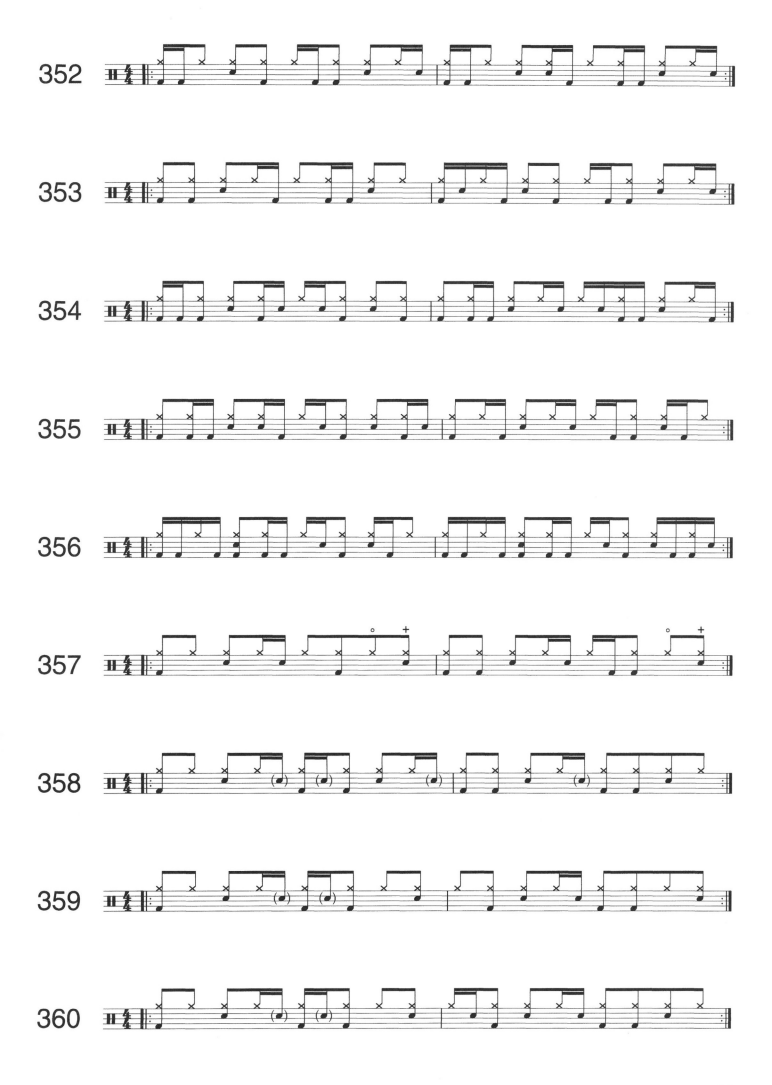

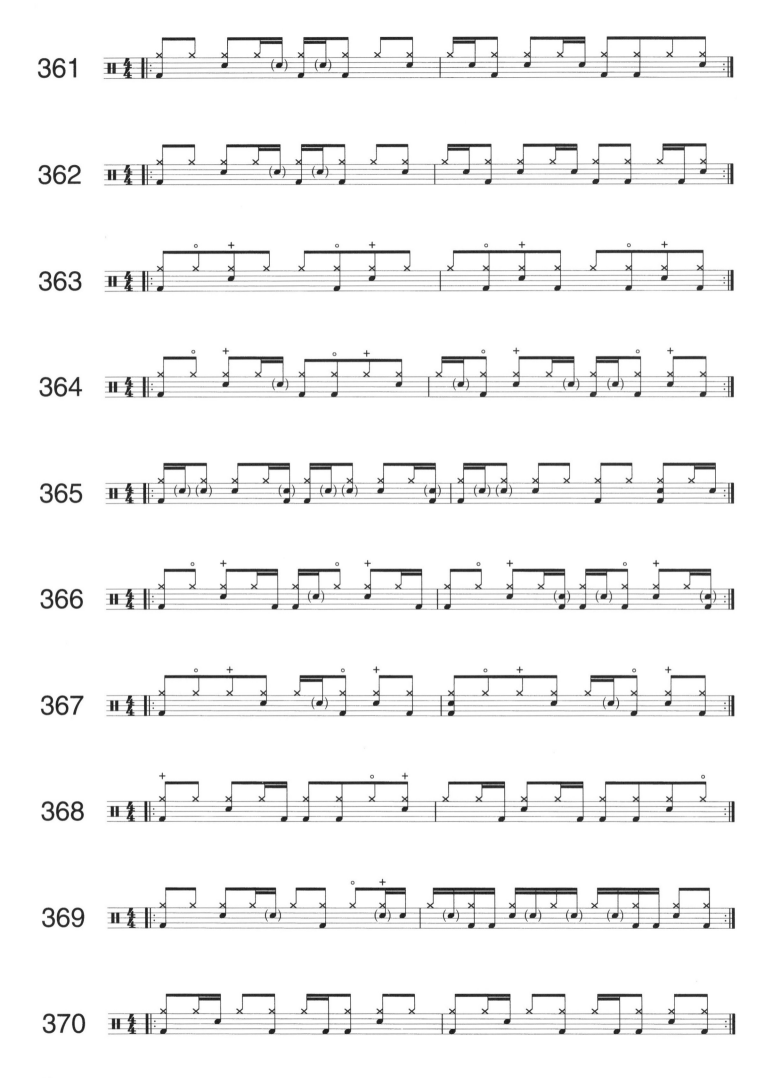

Punk & Speed Metal

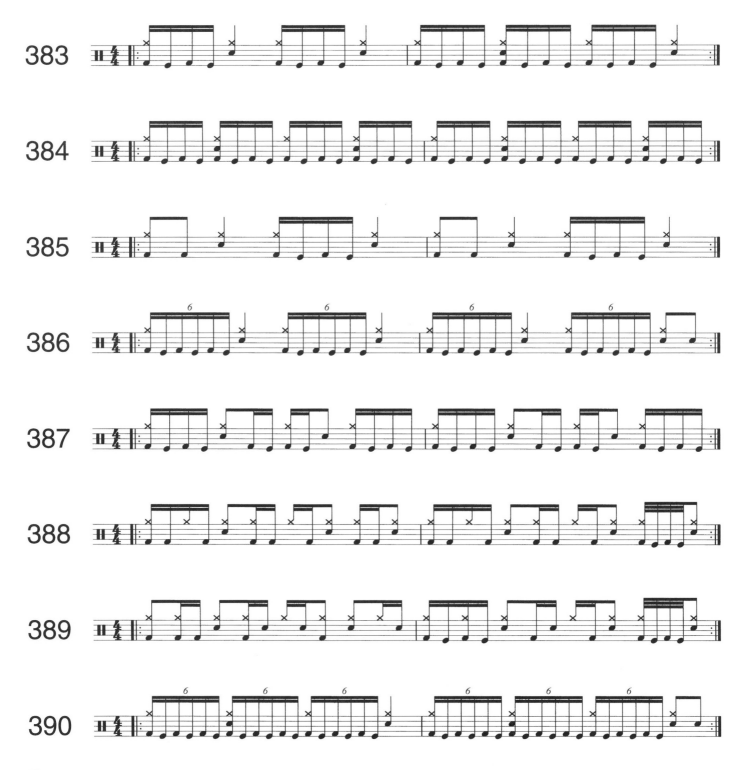

Double Bass

Blues, 12/8, Shuffles (triplets)

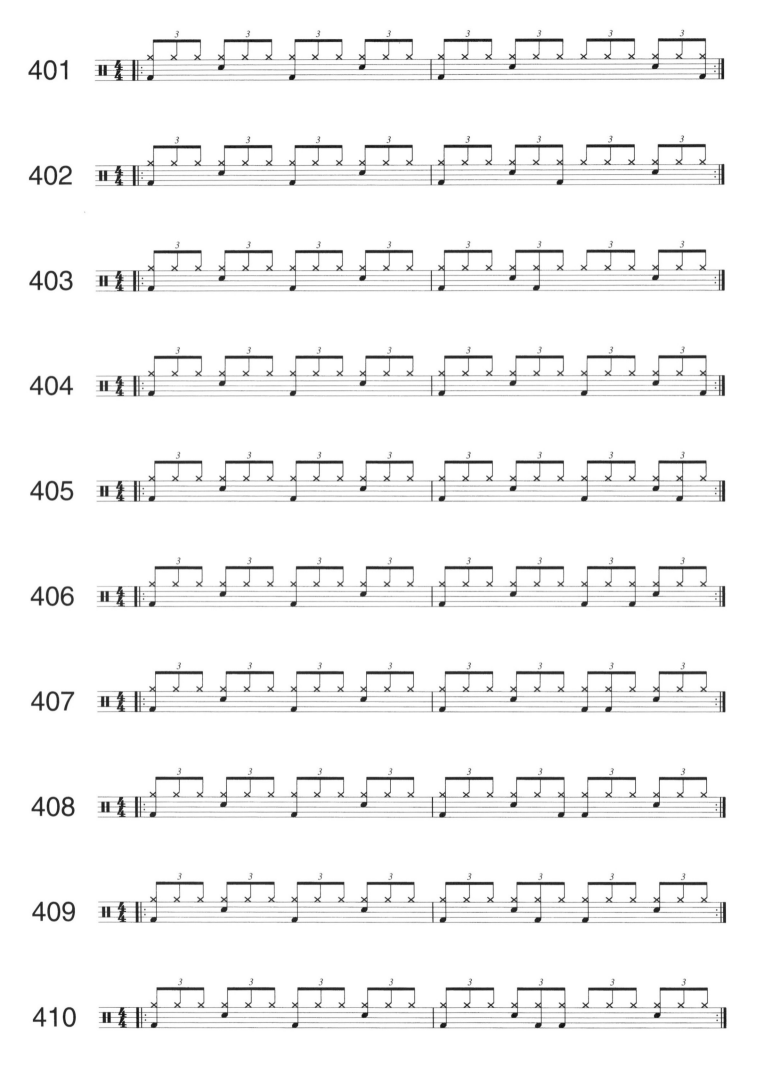

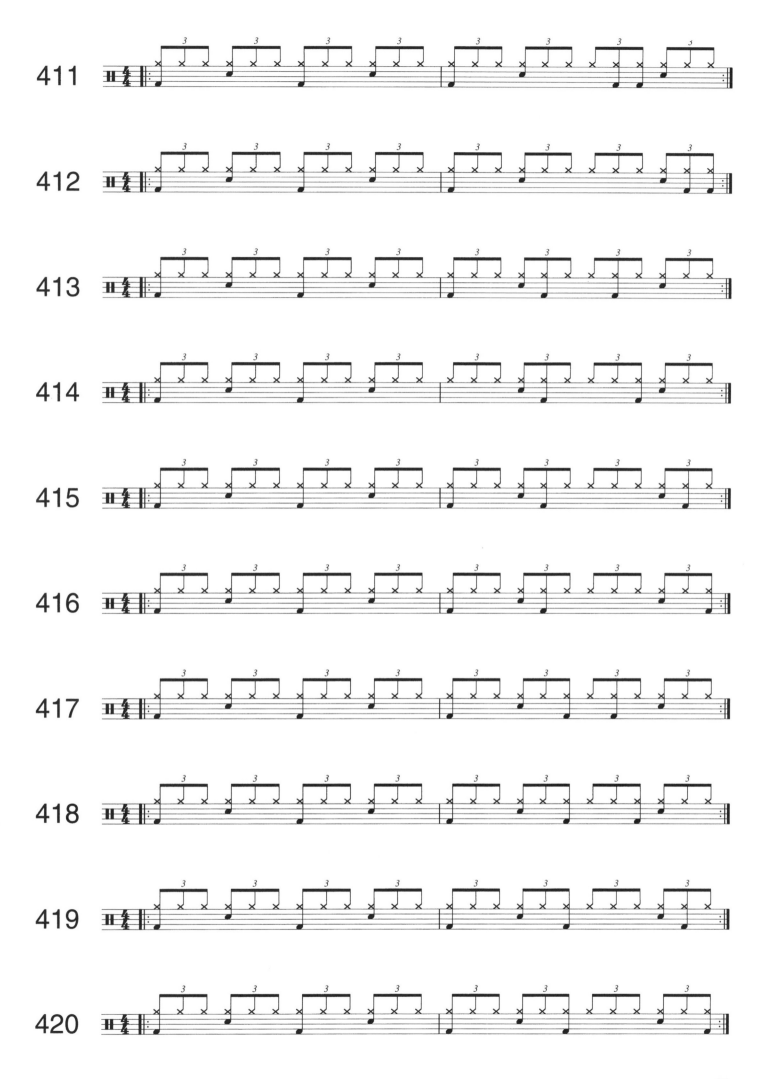

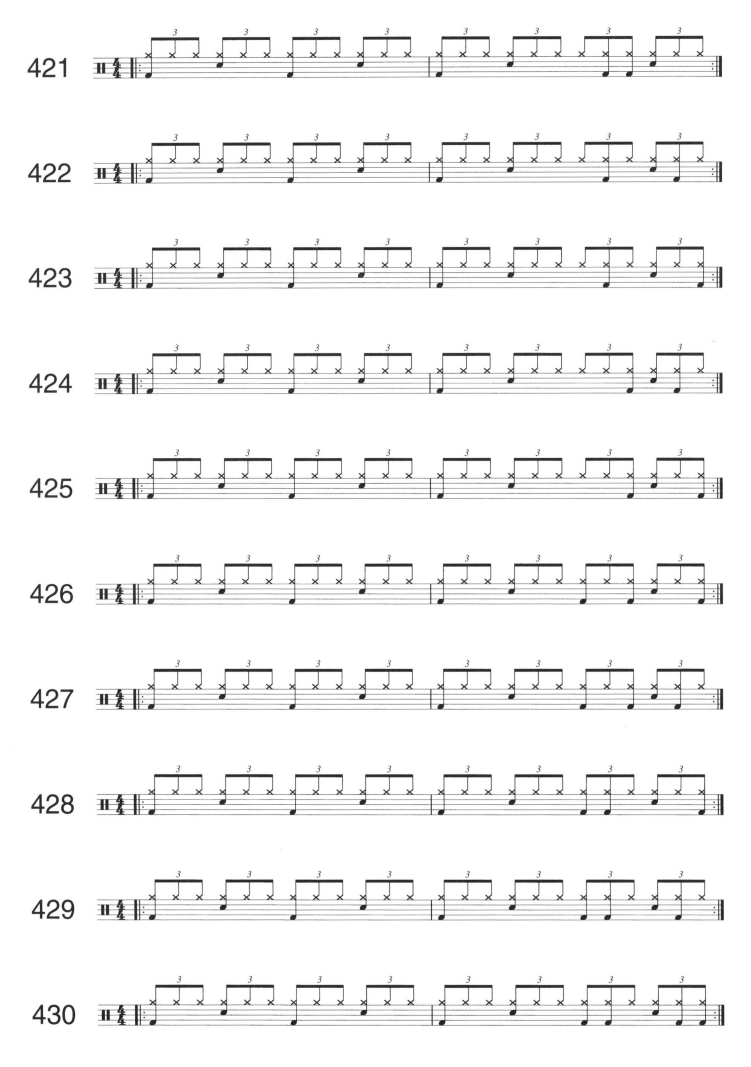

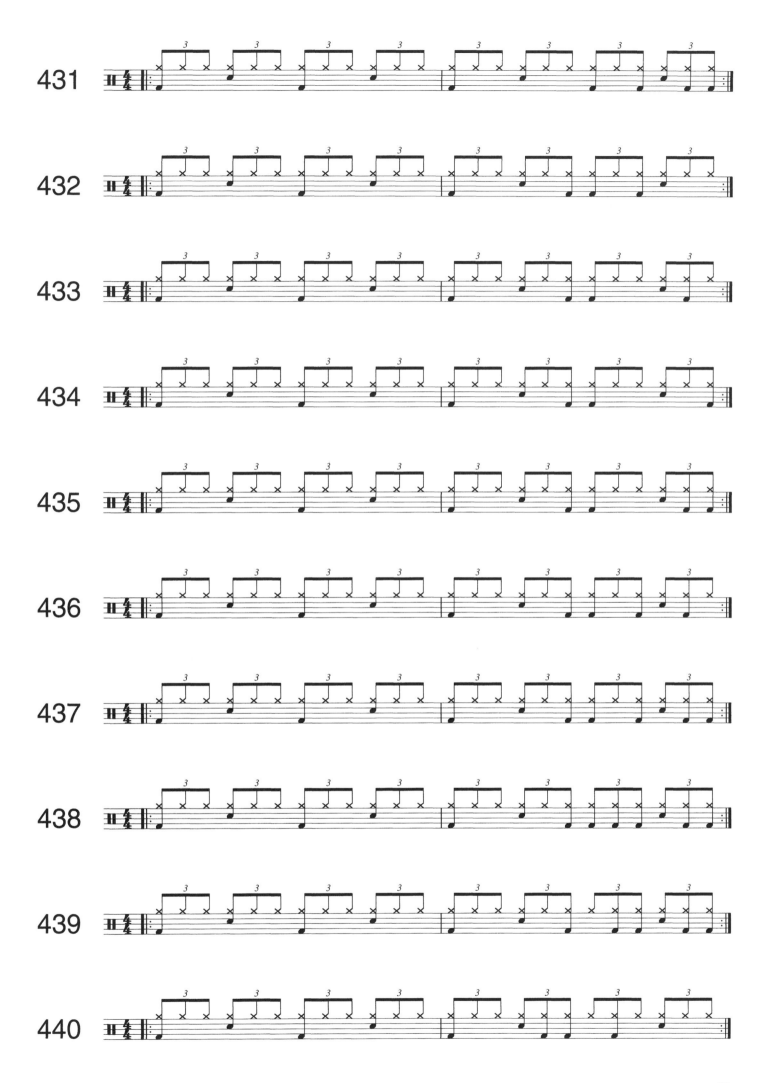

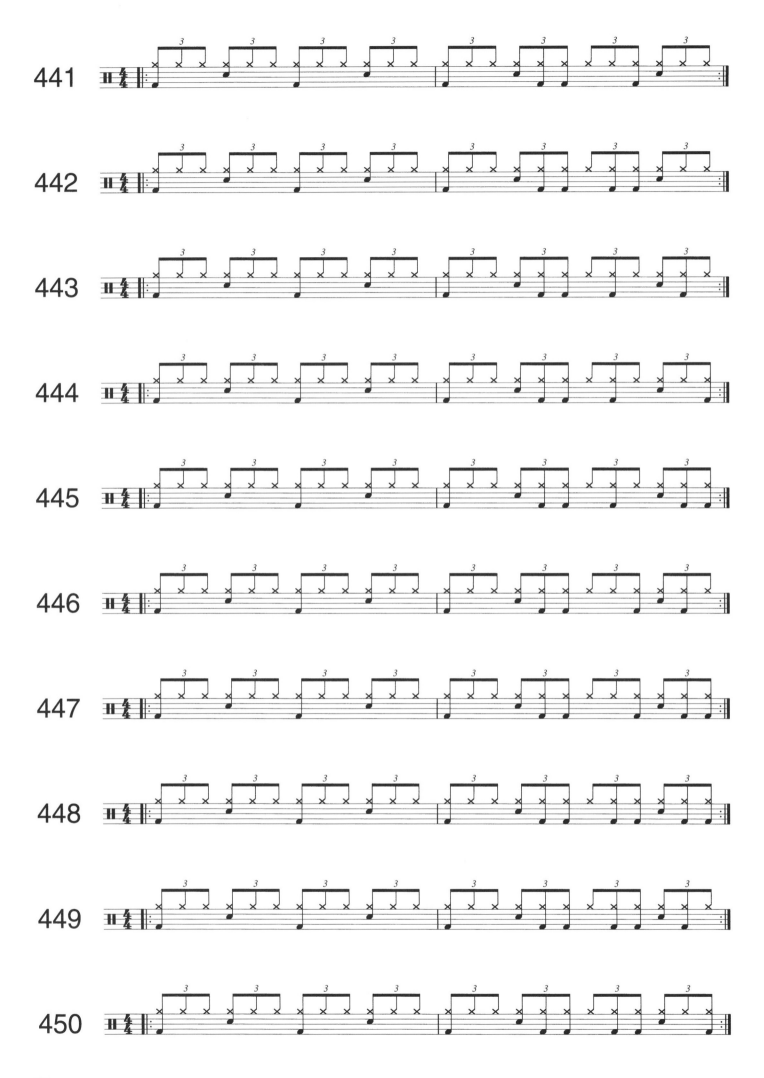

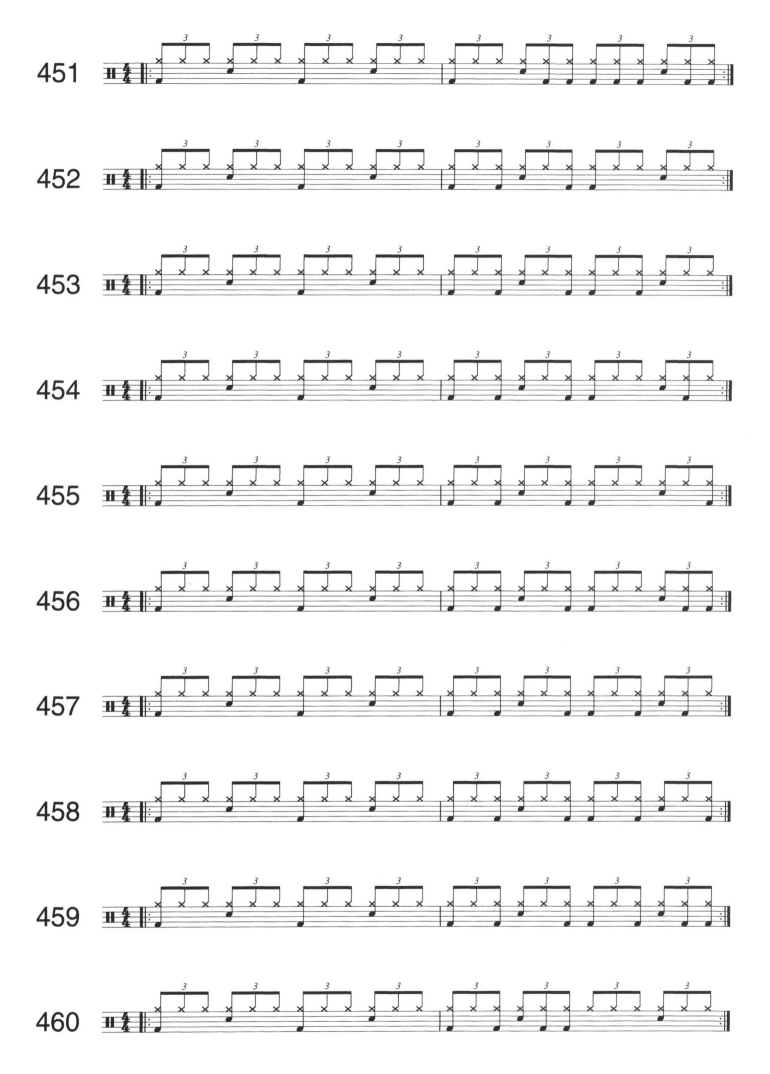

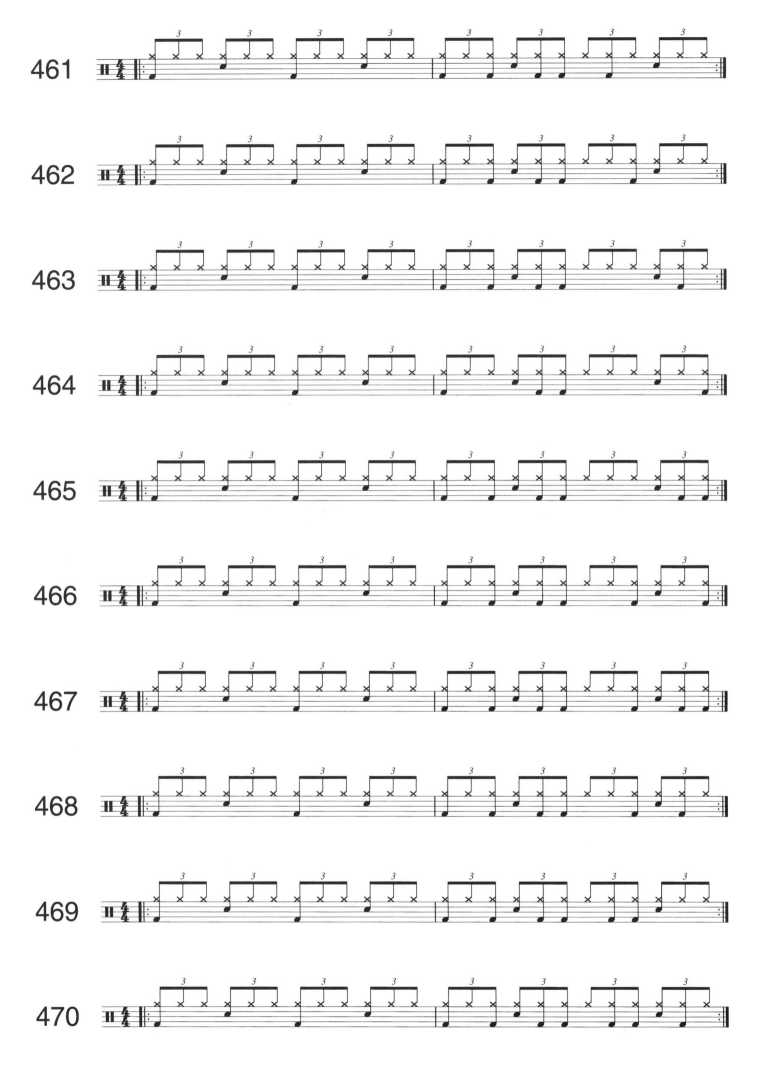

461

462

463

464

465

466

467

468

469

470

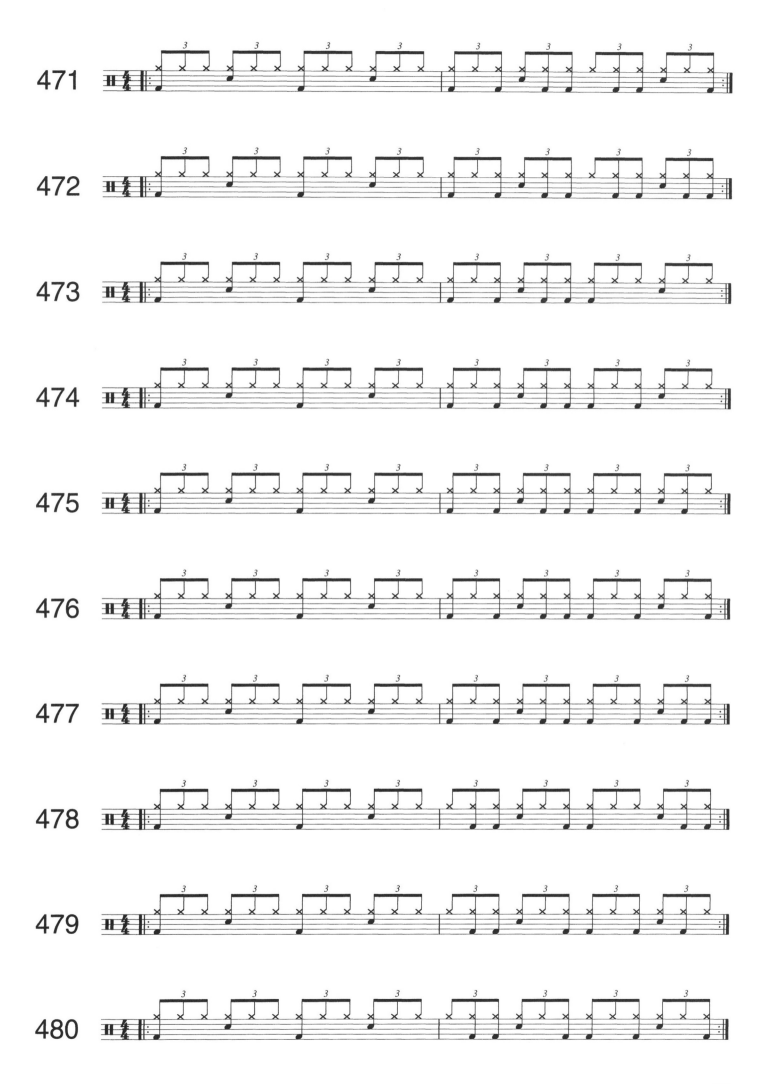

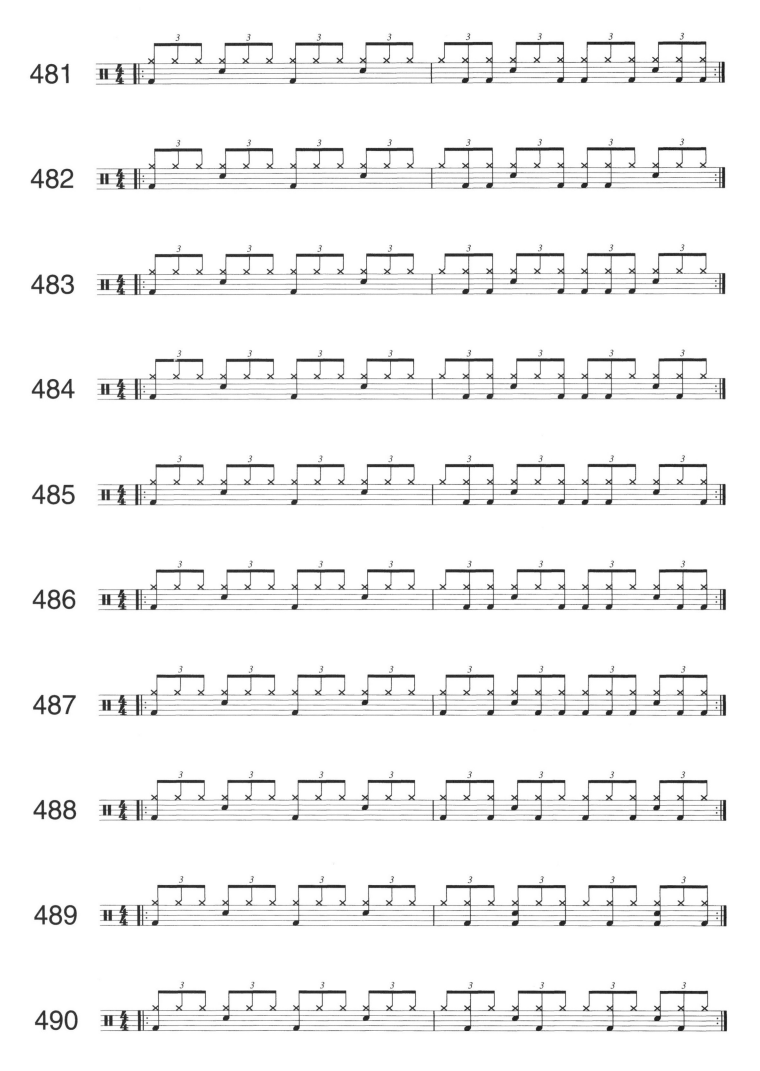

481

482

483

484

485

486

487

488

489

490

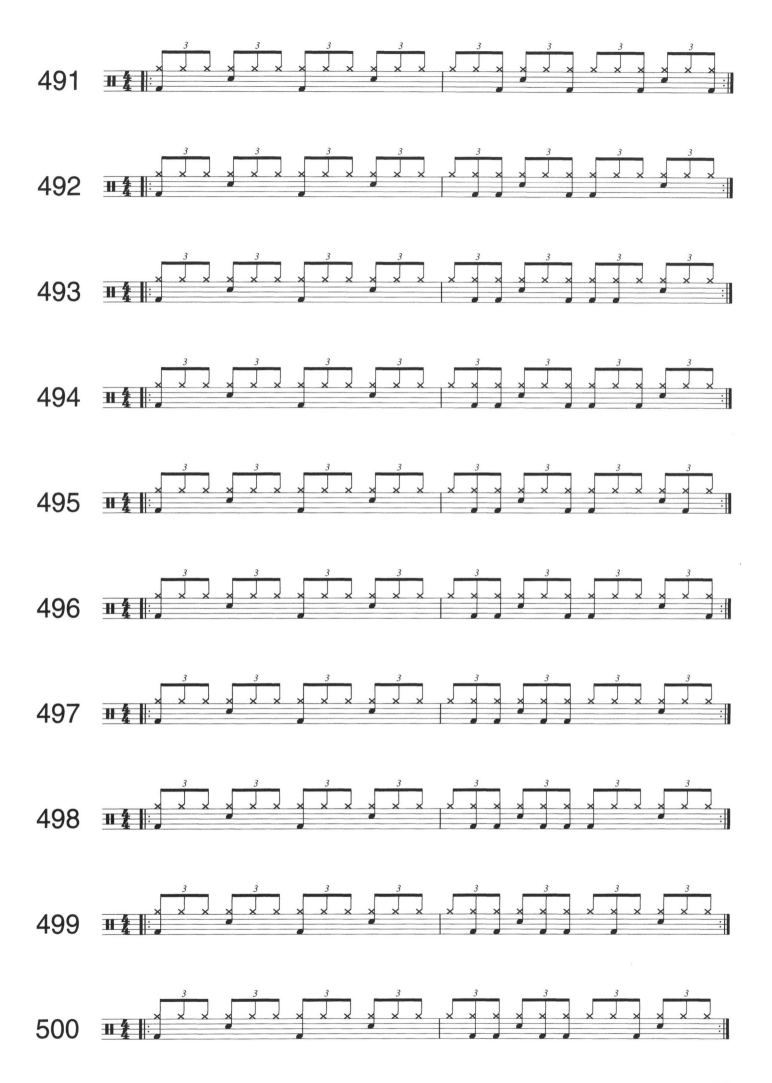

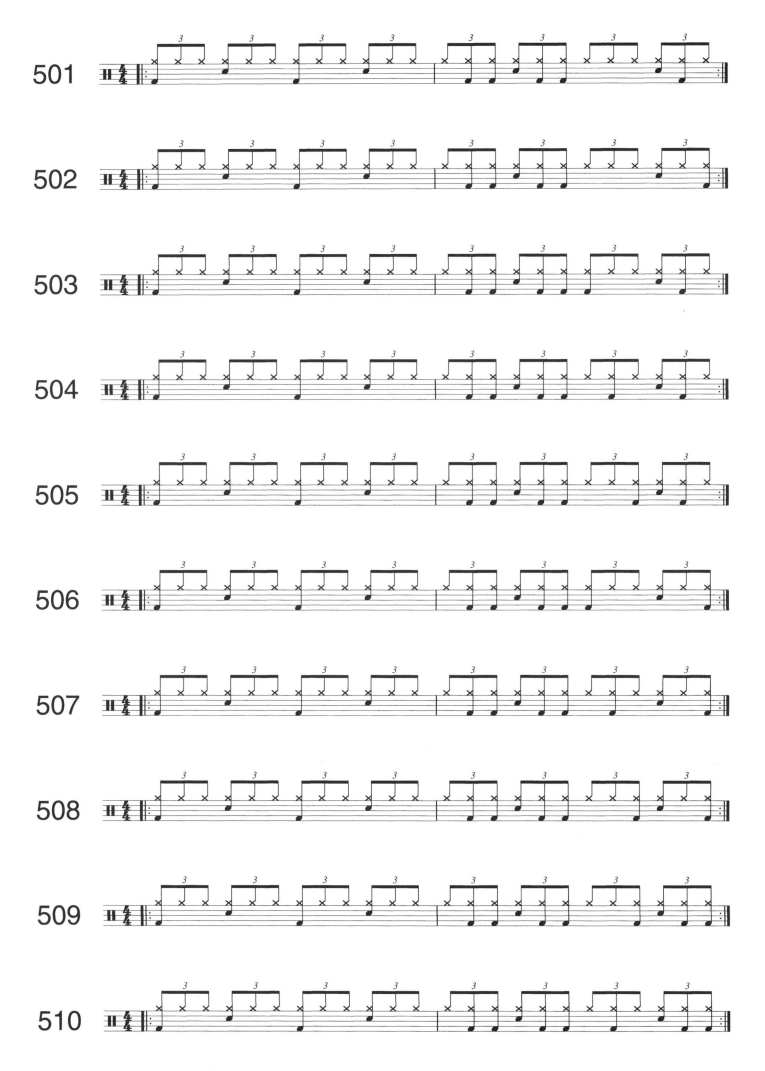

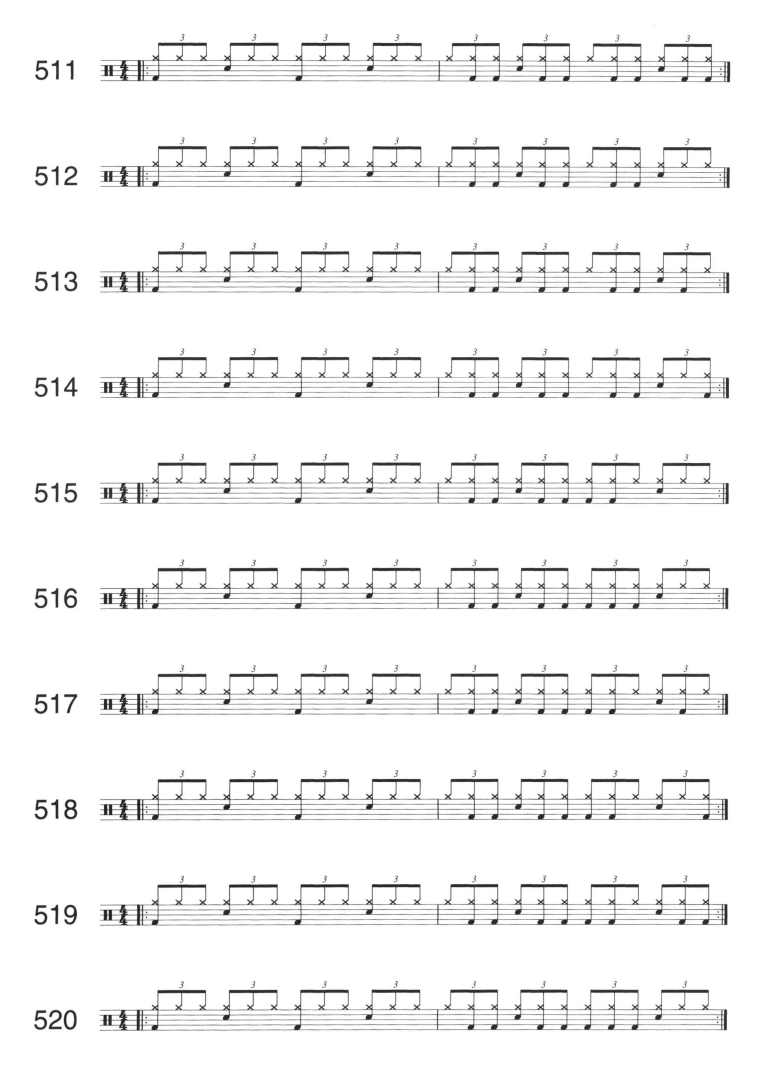

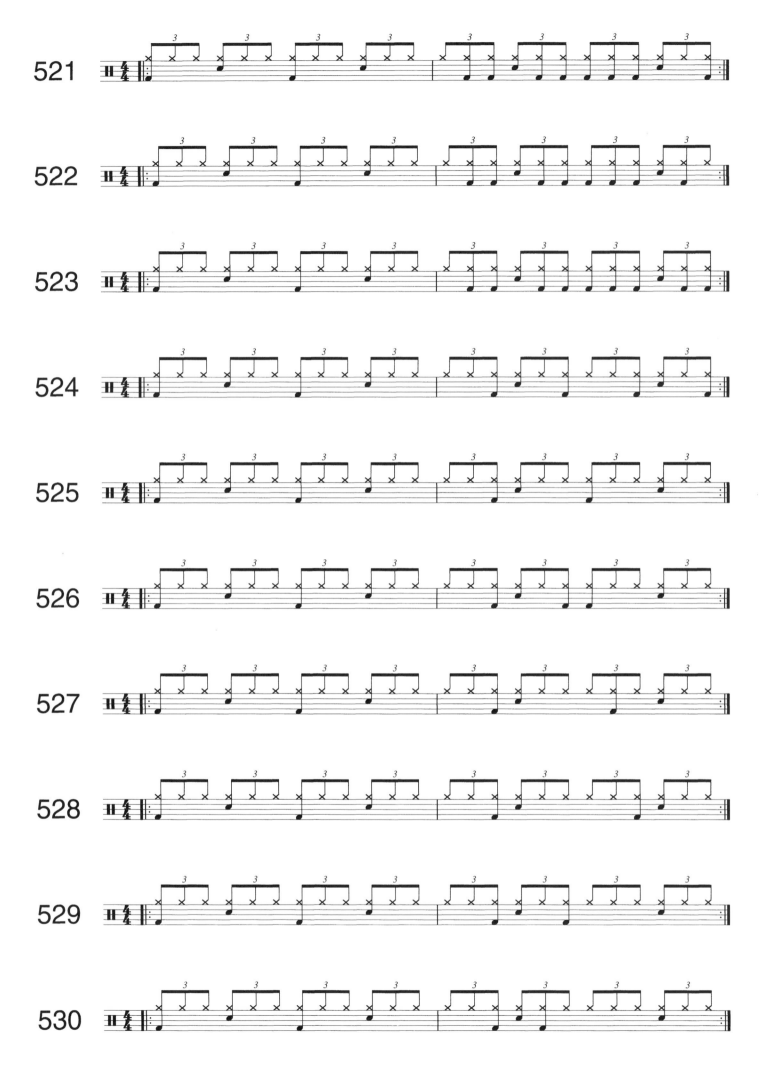

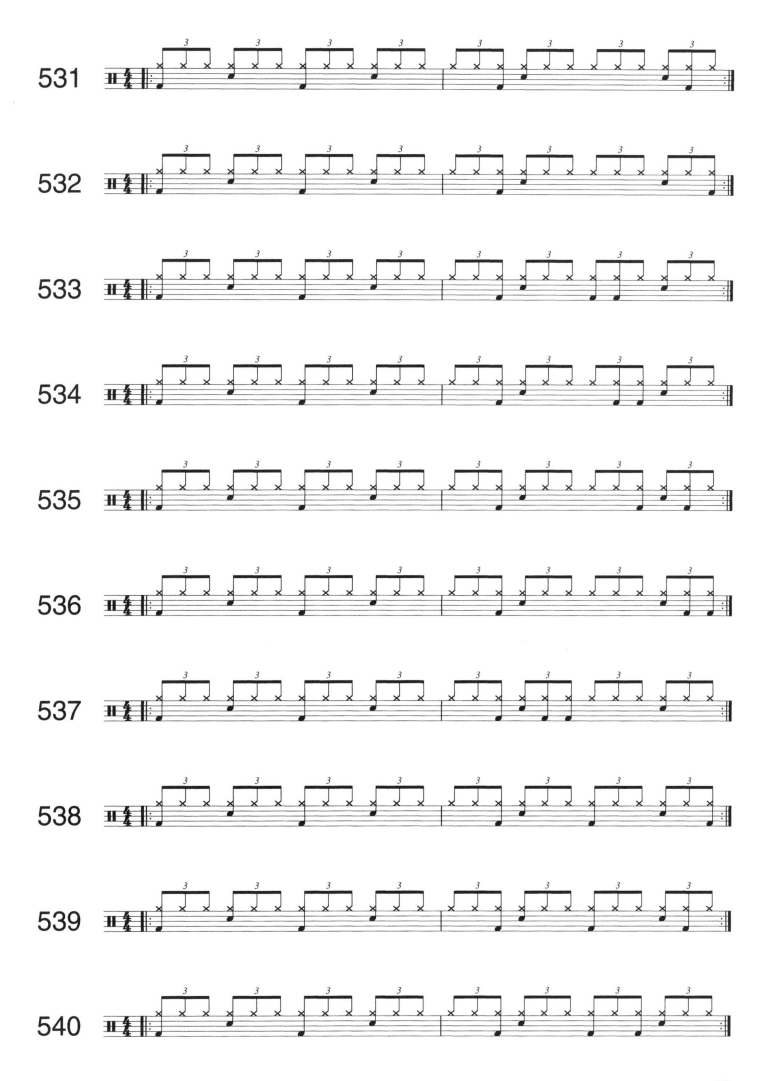

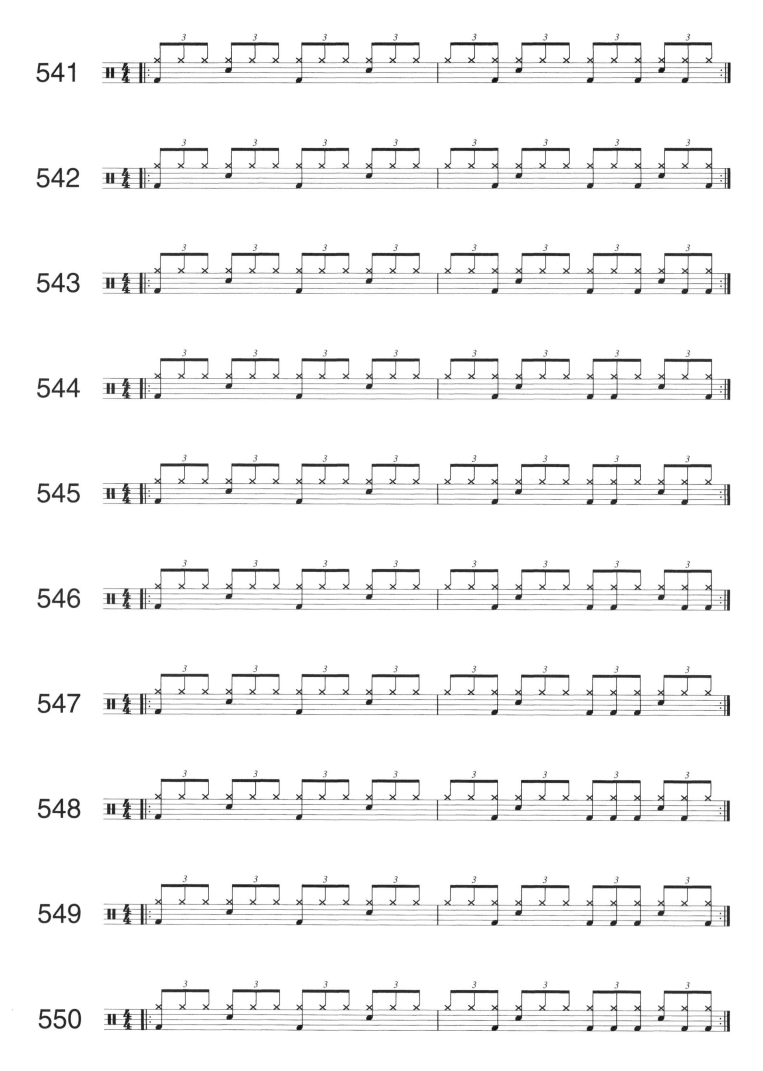

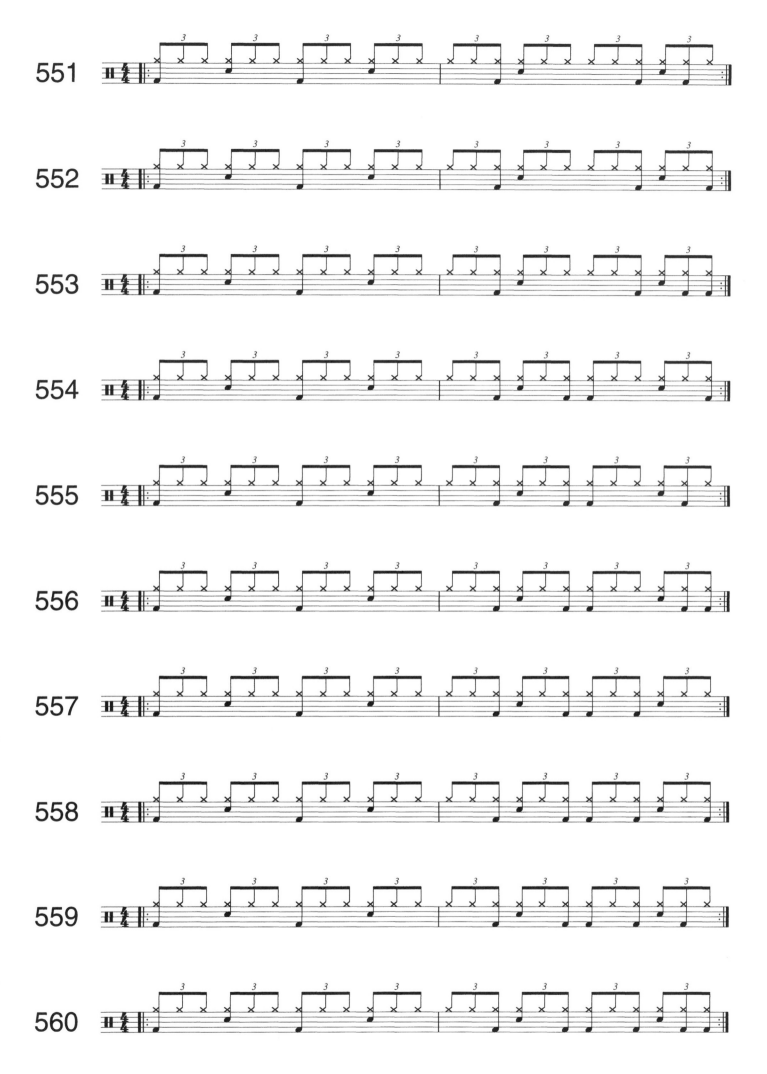

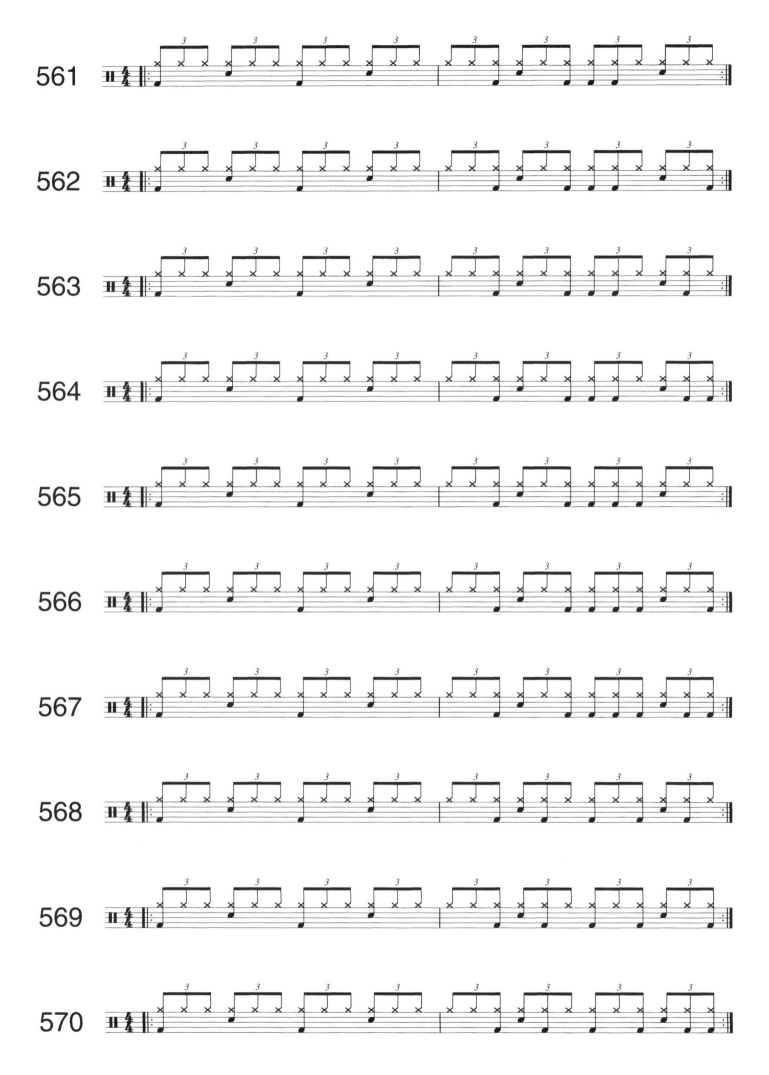

561

562

563

564

565

566

567

568

569

570

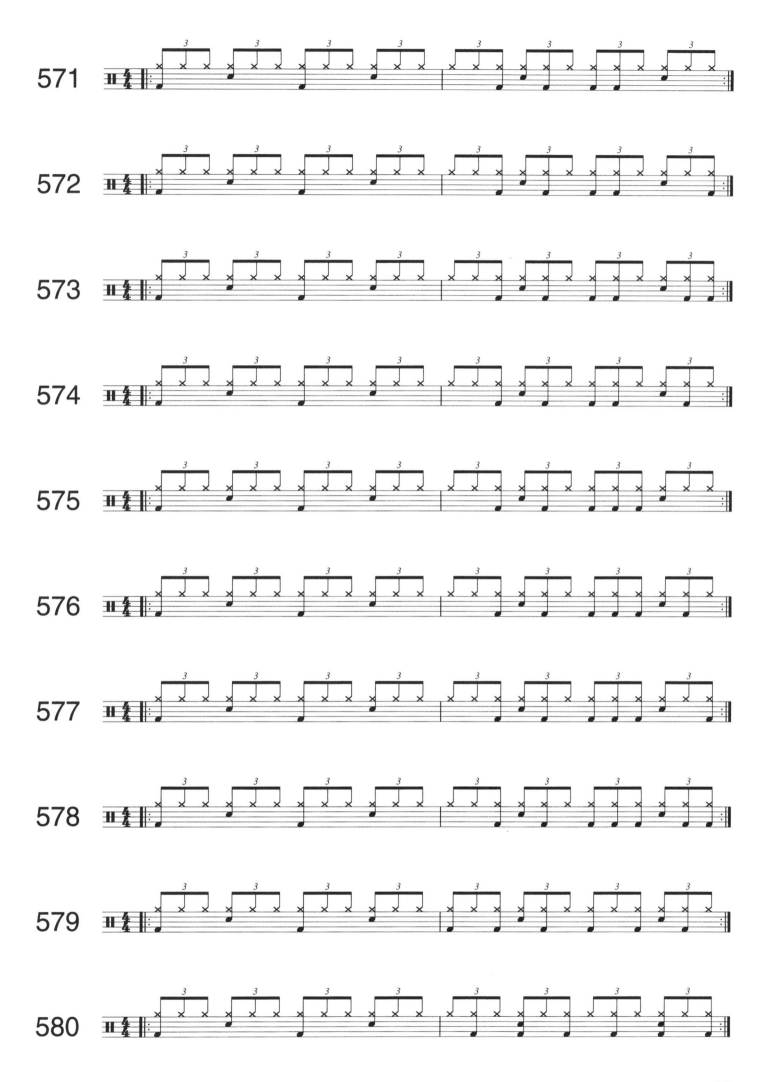

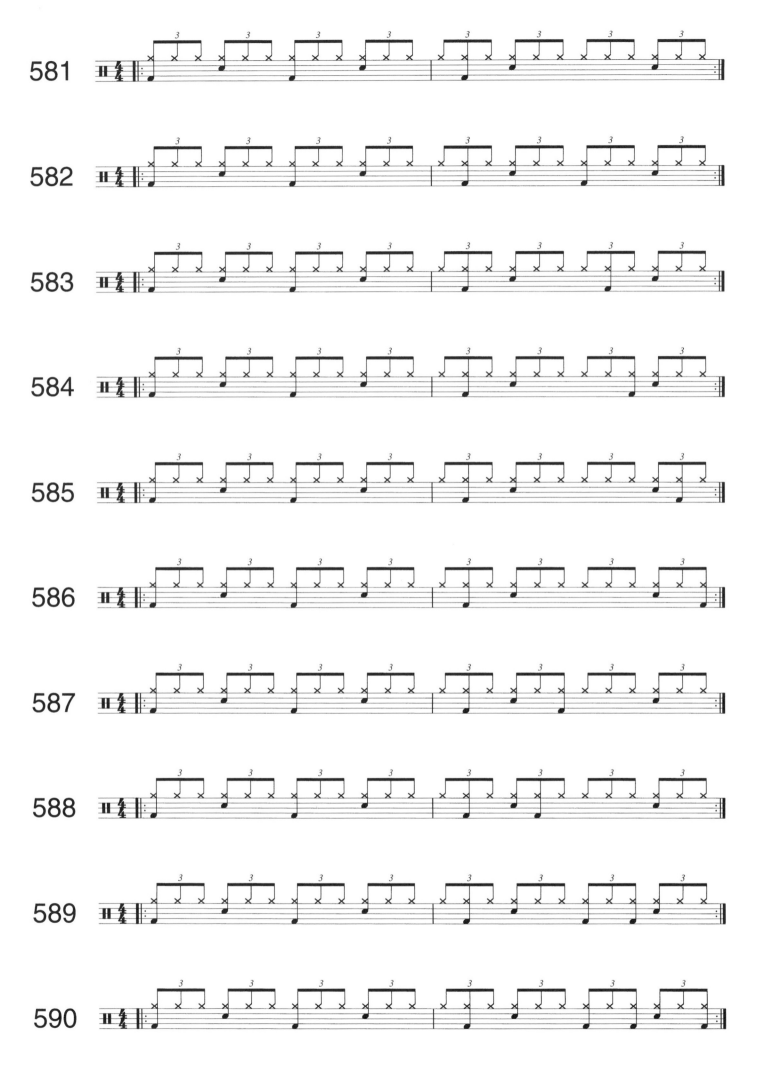

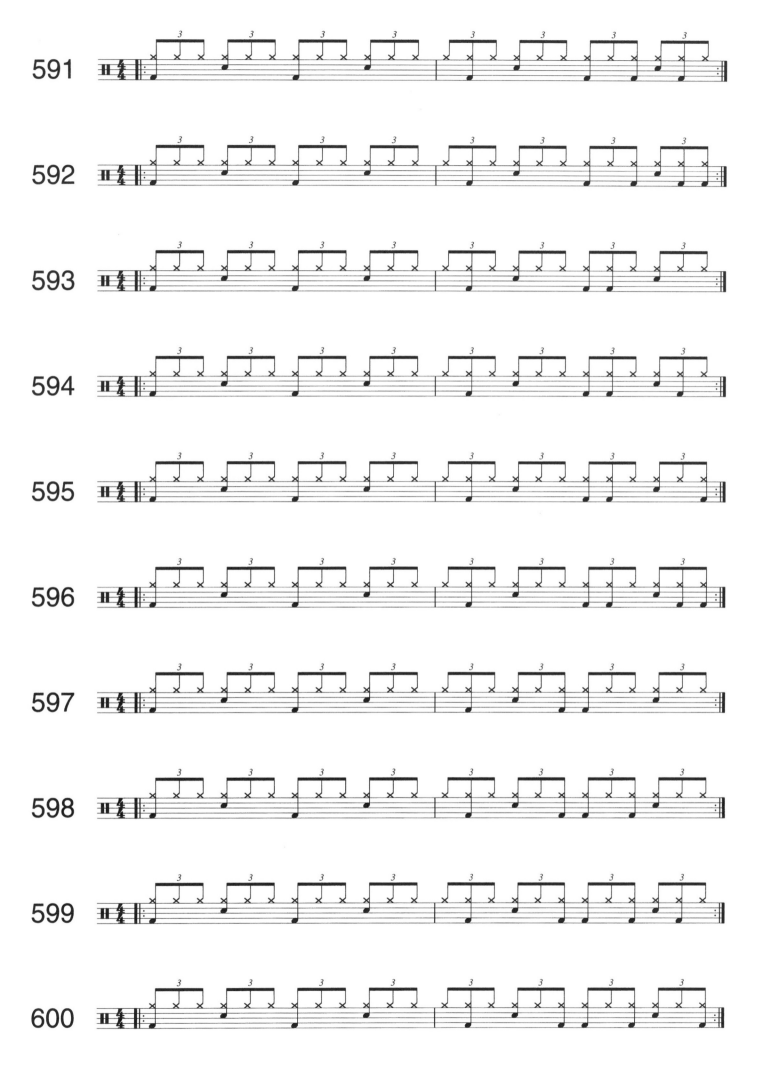

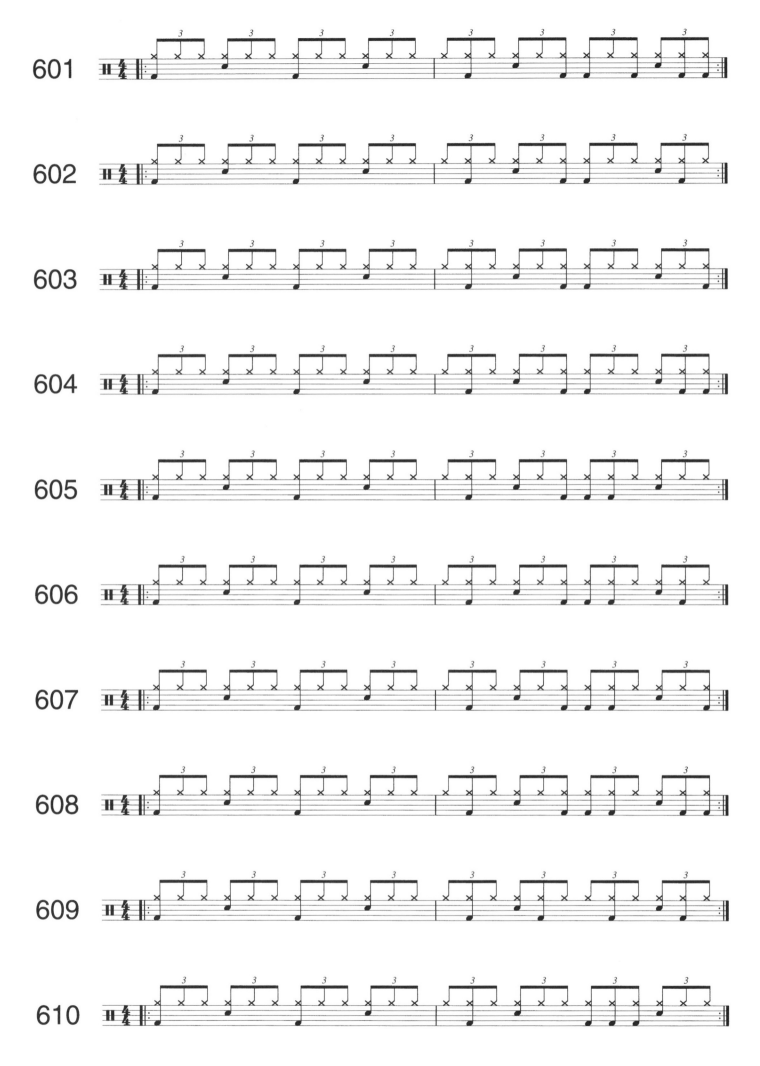

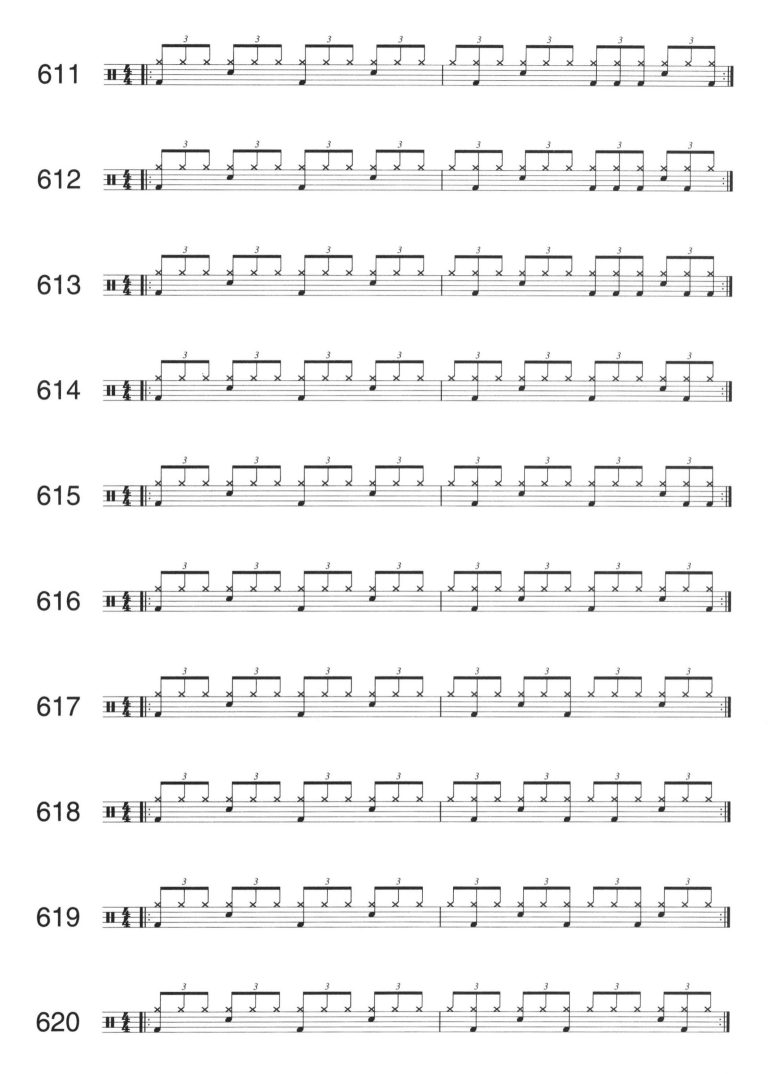

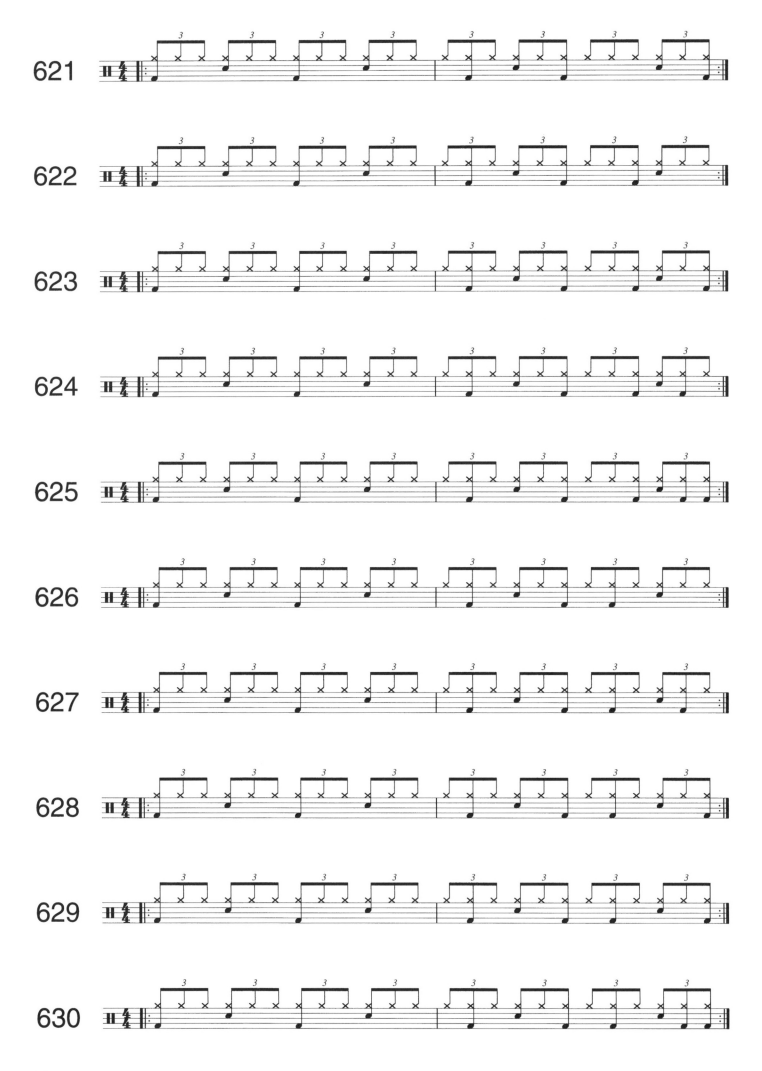

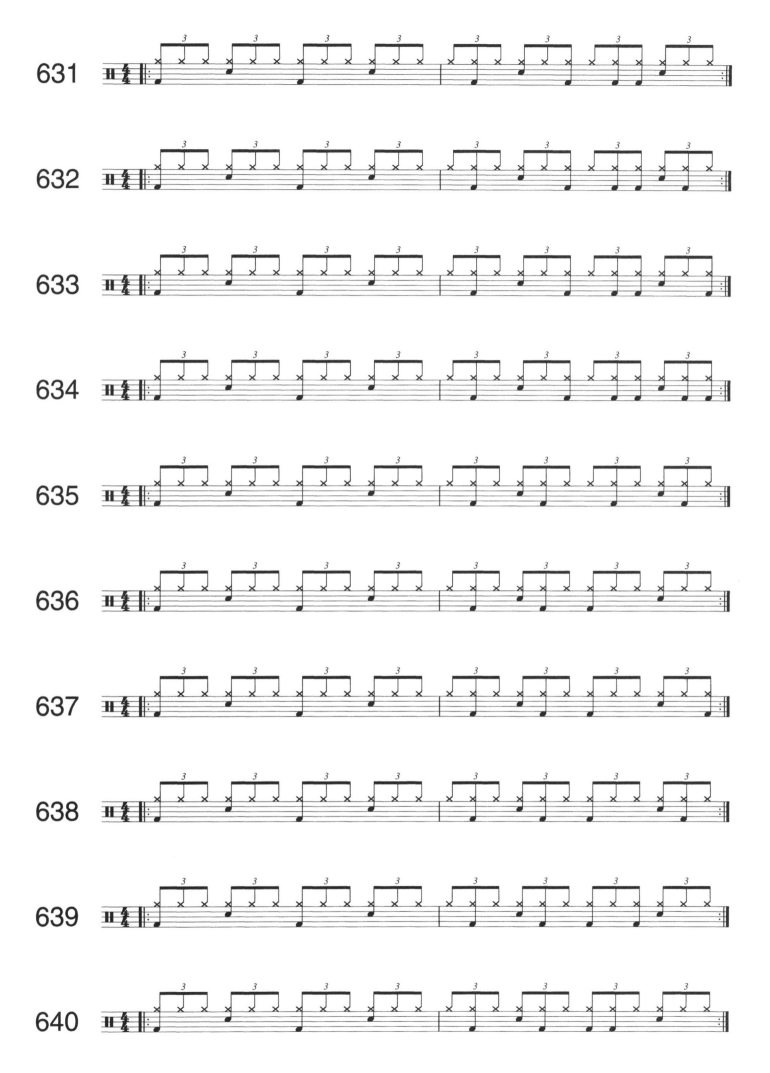

641

642

643

644

645

646

Applications

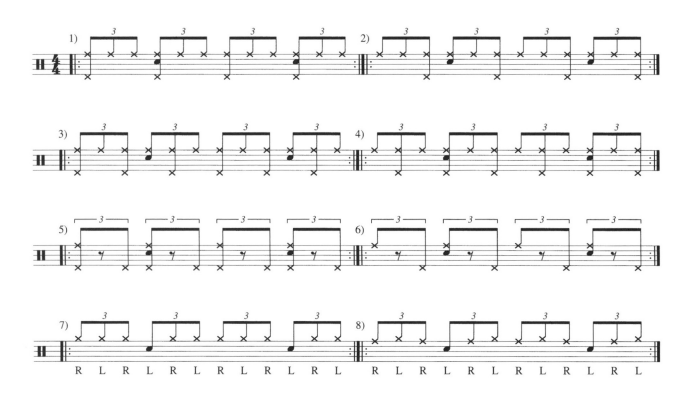

R L R L R L R L R L R L R L   R L R L R L R L R L R L R L

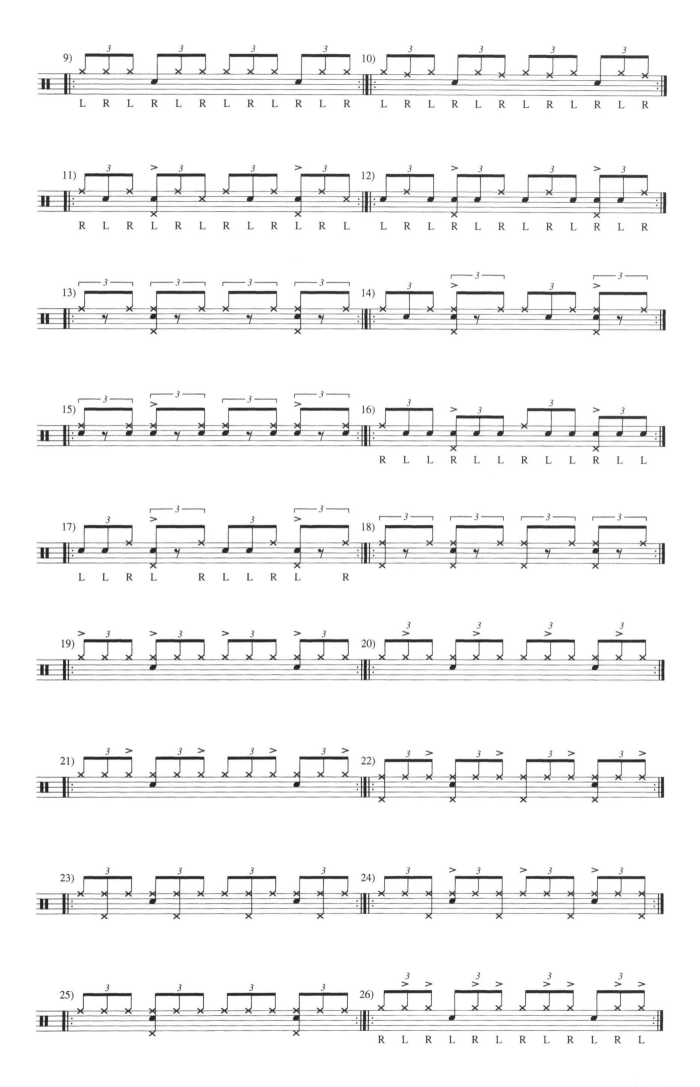

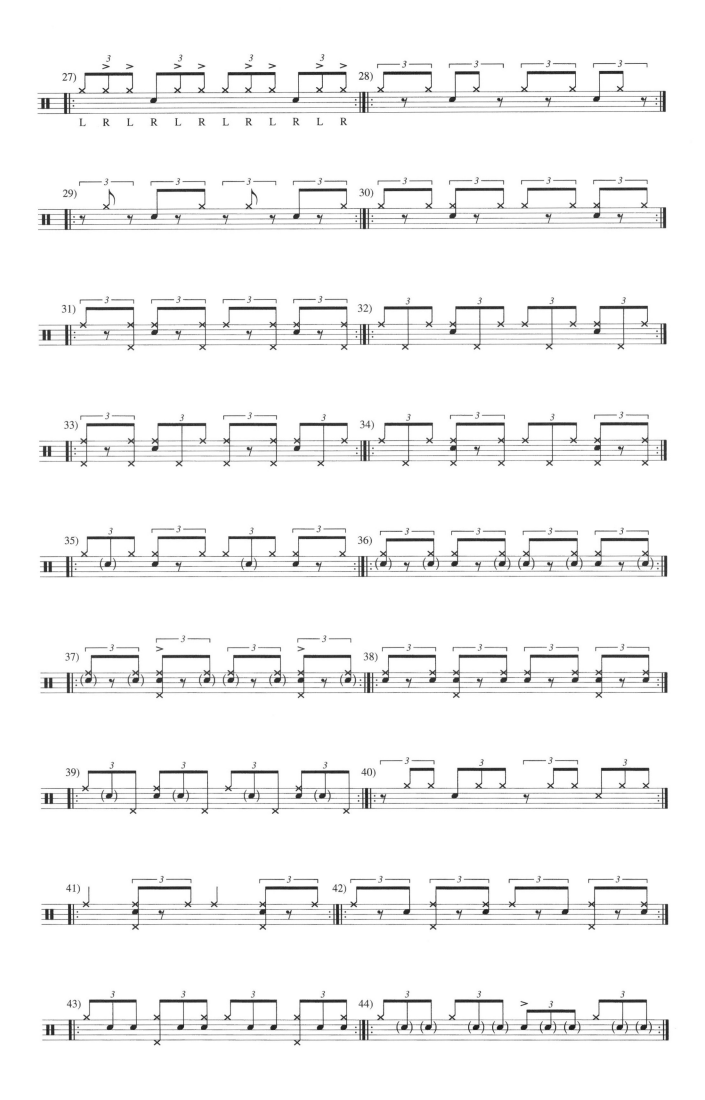

Various Blues, 12/8, Zydeco & Shuffle Grooves

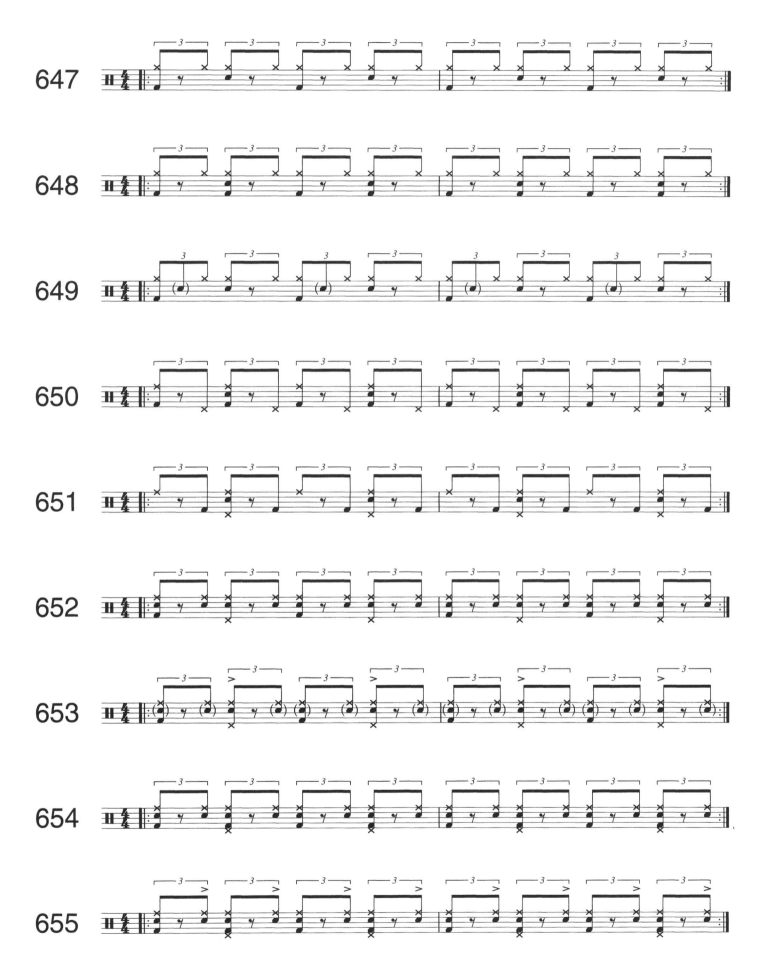

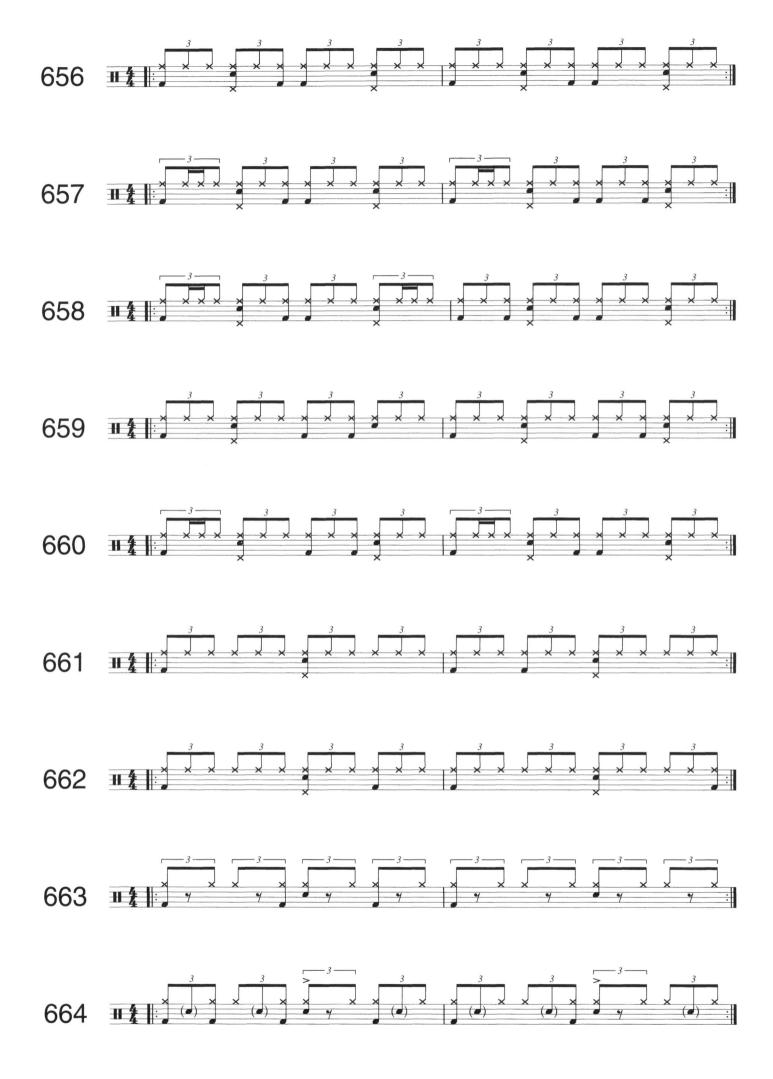

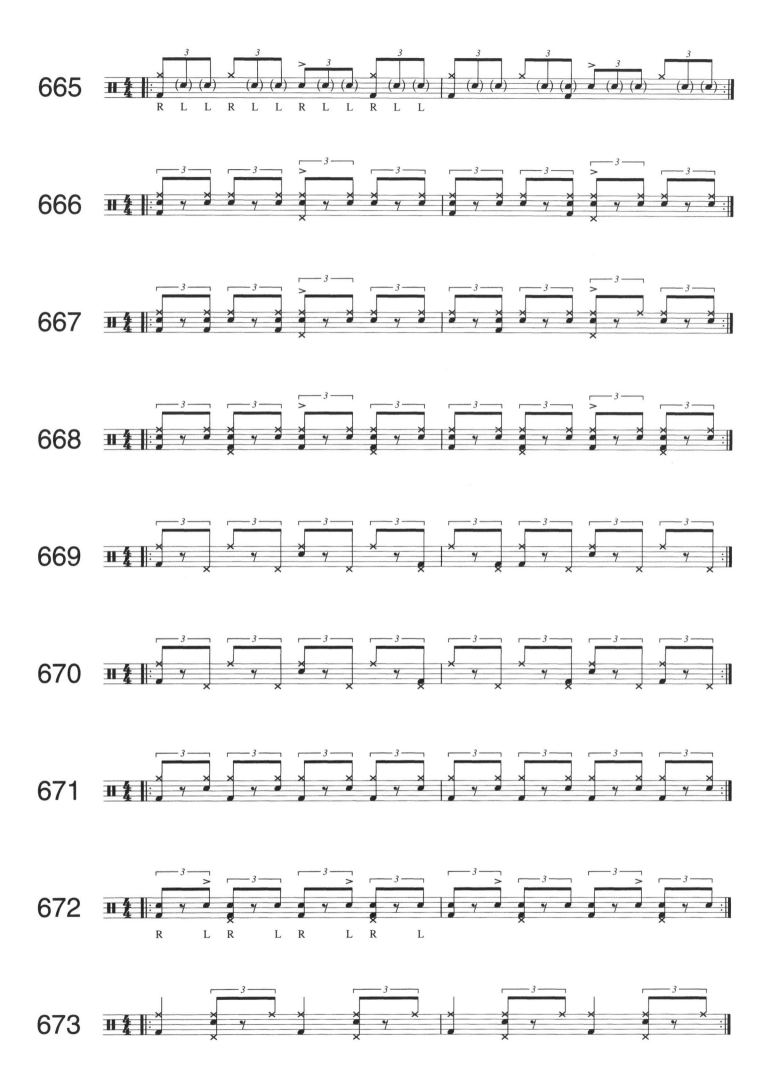

Jazz

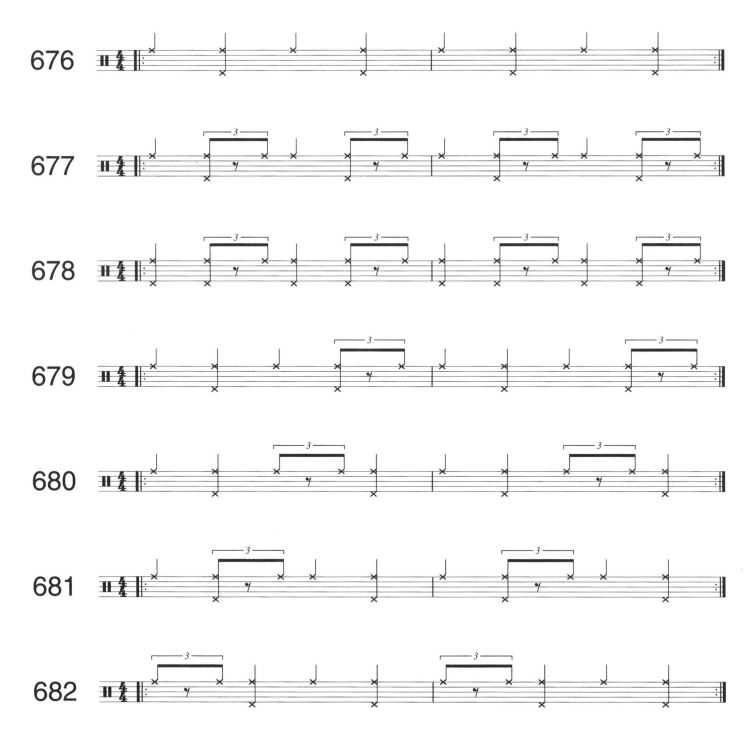

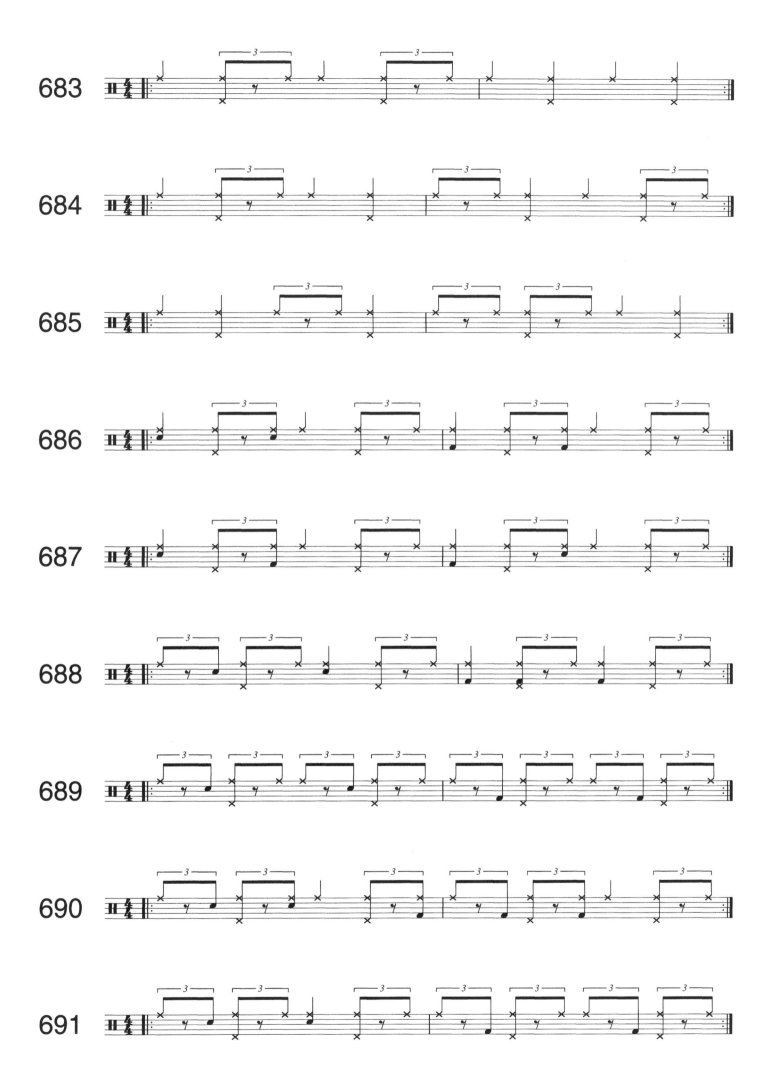

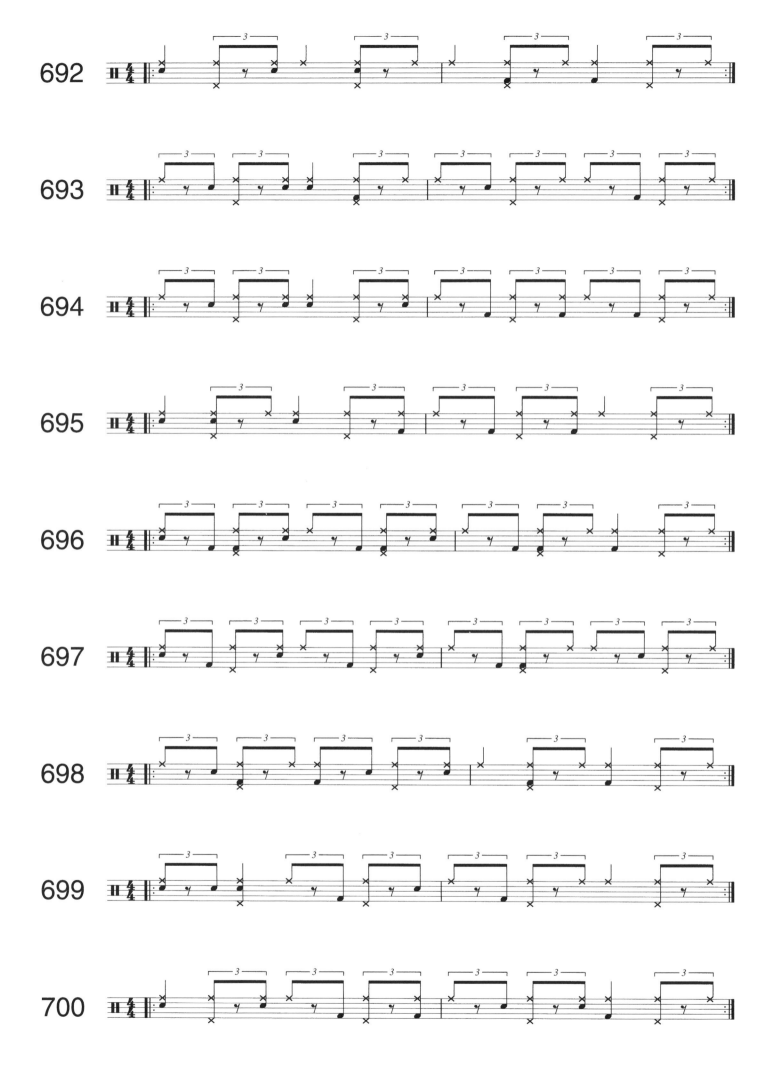

711

712

713

714

715

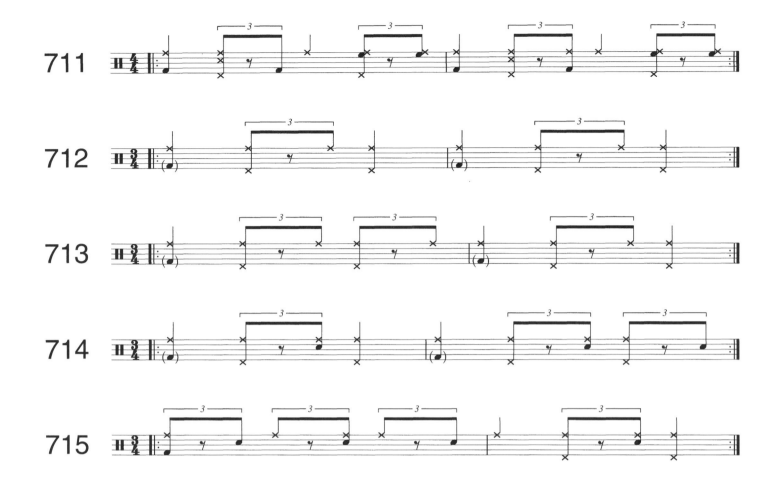

Bolero

716

717

718

719

720

American Bolero

731

732

733

734

735

Argentine Tango

736

737

738

739

740

Spanish Tango

American Waltz

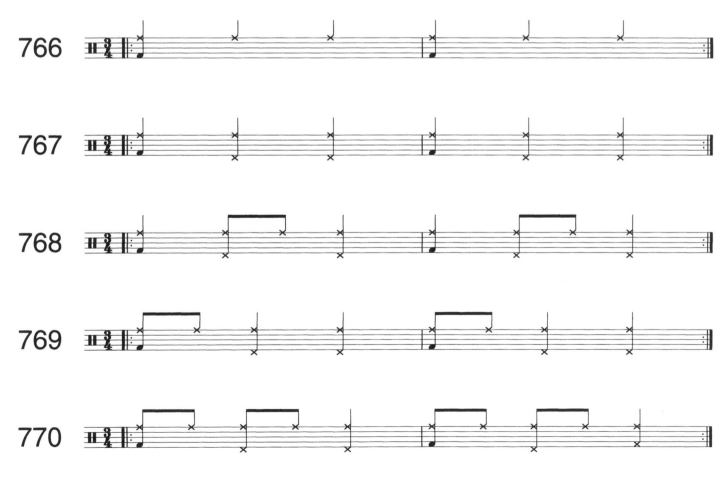

Viennese Waltz

Polka

Polka Mazurka

780

Jewish Frailach

781

782

783

Bulgar

784

785

786

787

Flamenco

788

789

Jota

790

Jorpa

791

Spanish Waltz

792

Valsa

793

Italian Tarantella

794

Irish Reel

795

Greek 7/8

796

797

798

799

800

Greek 9/8

801

802

803

804

805

Bossa Nova w/ Bossa Clave

806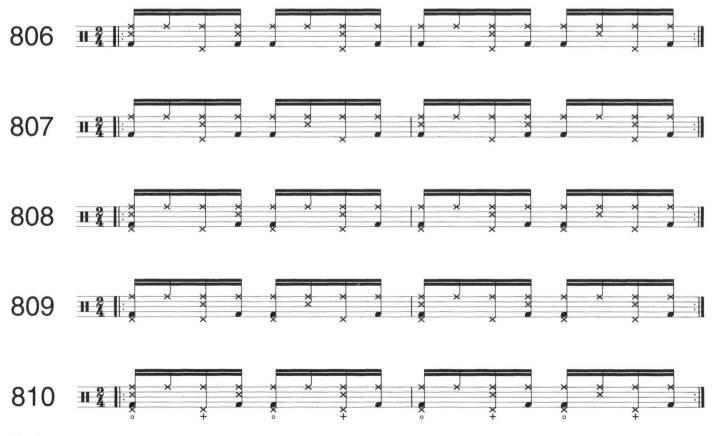

807

808

809

810

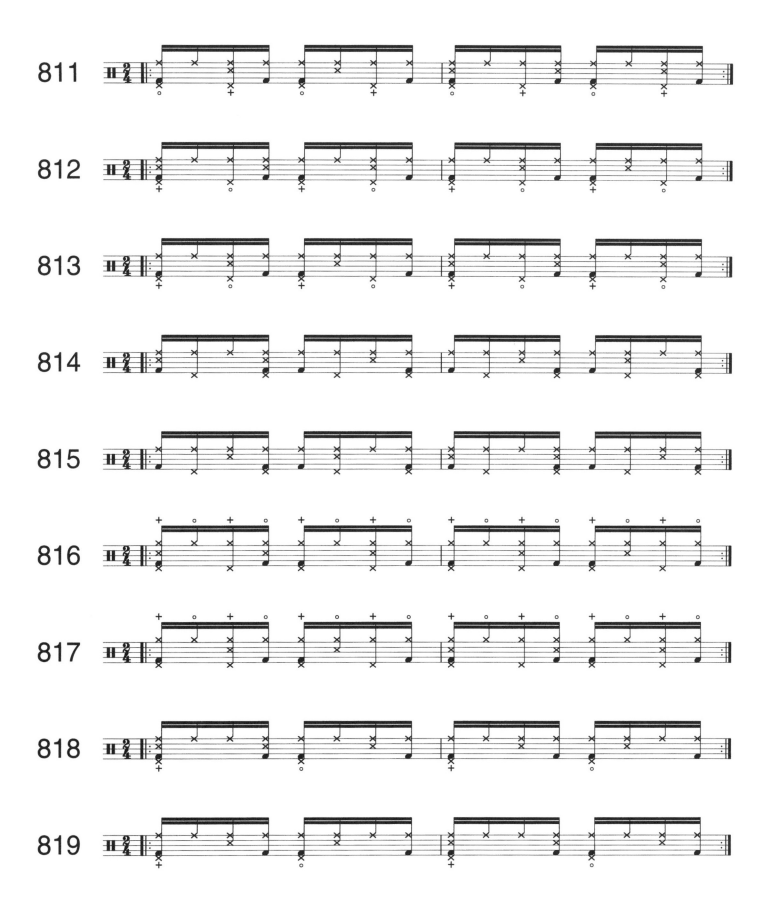

Bossa Nova w/ Son Clave

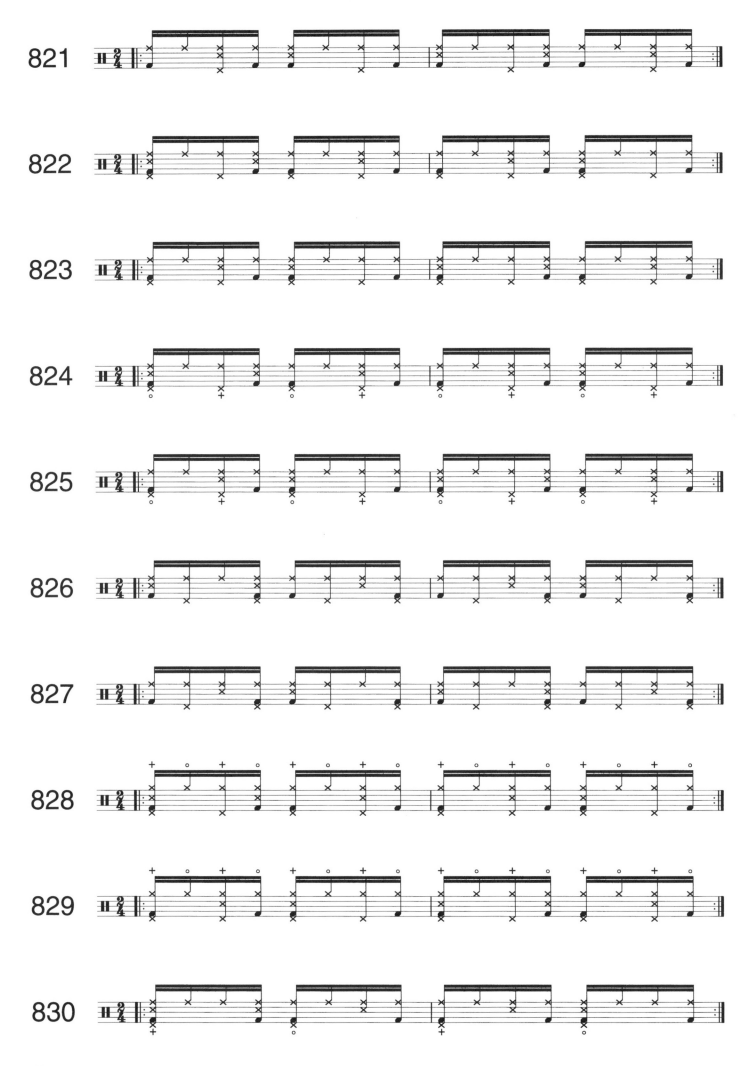

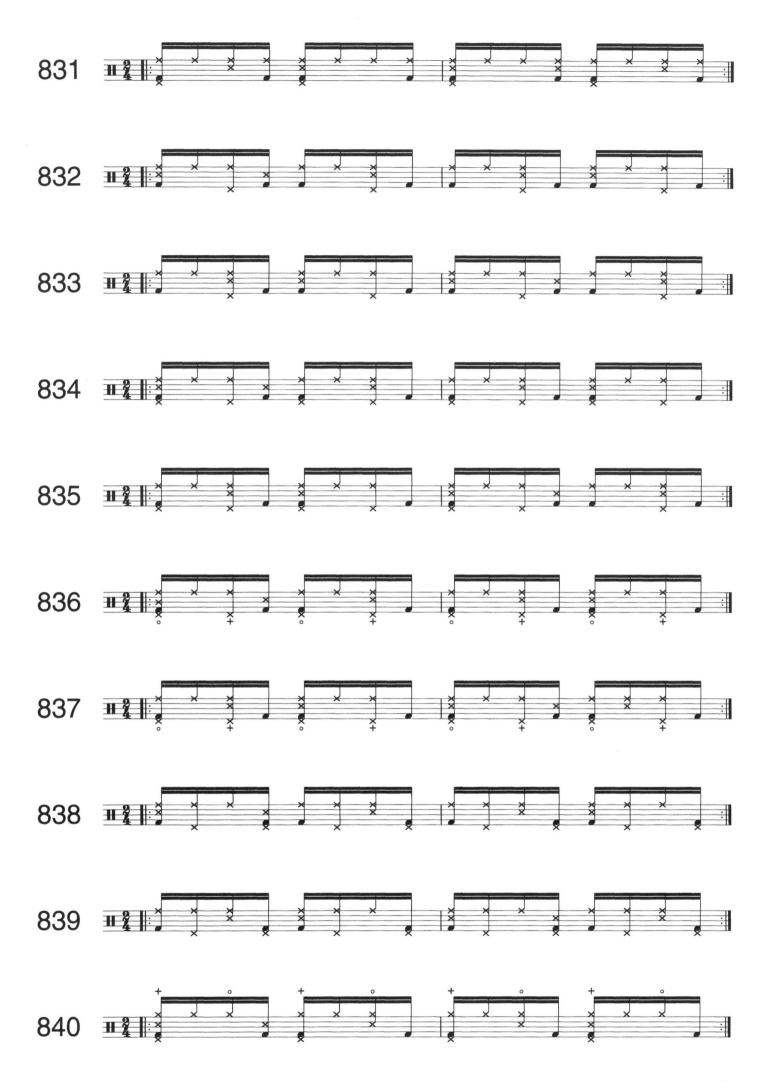

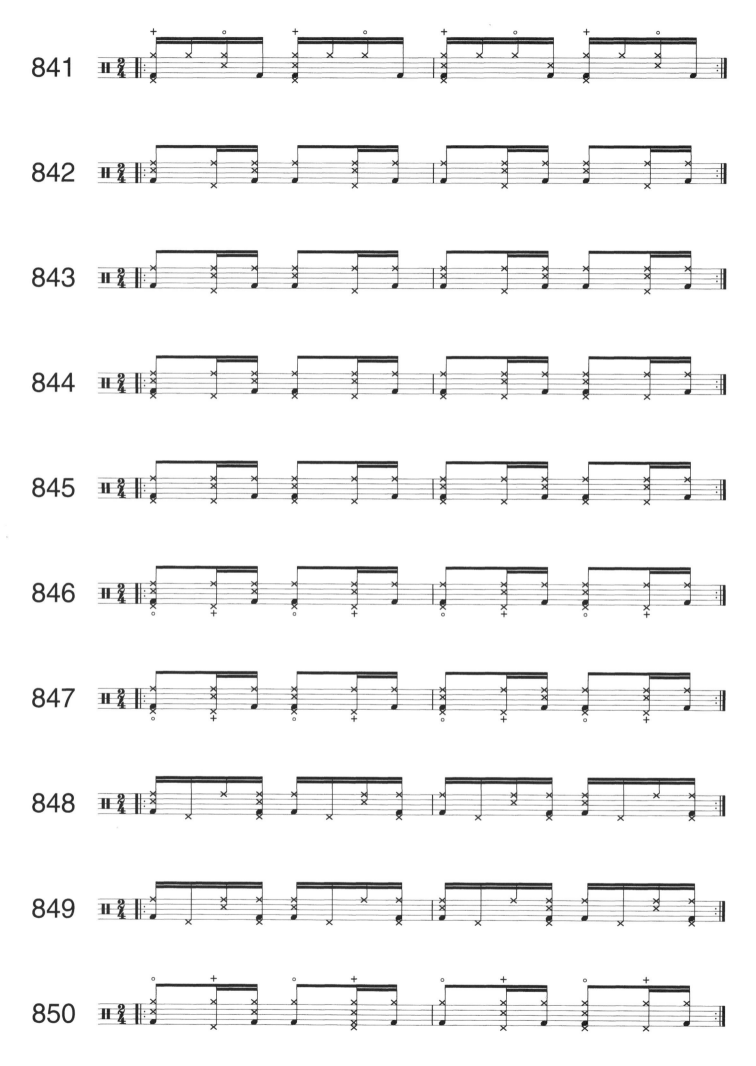

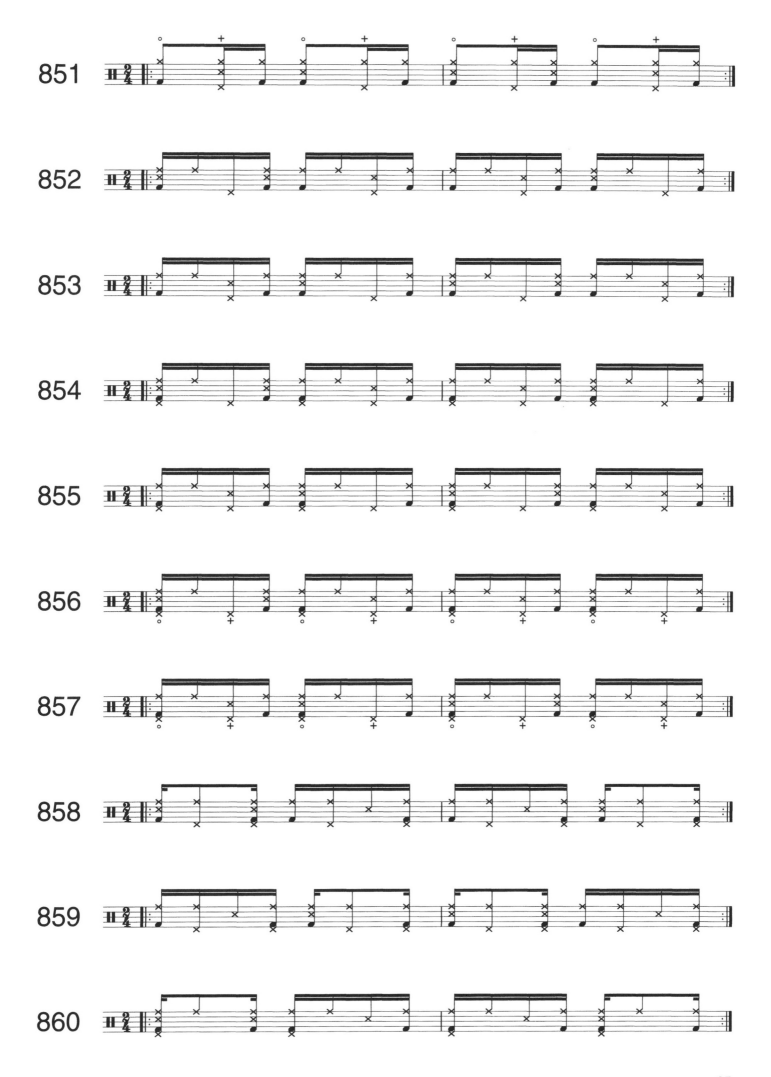

Bossa Nova w/ Rhumba Clave

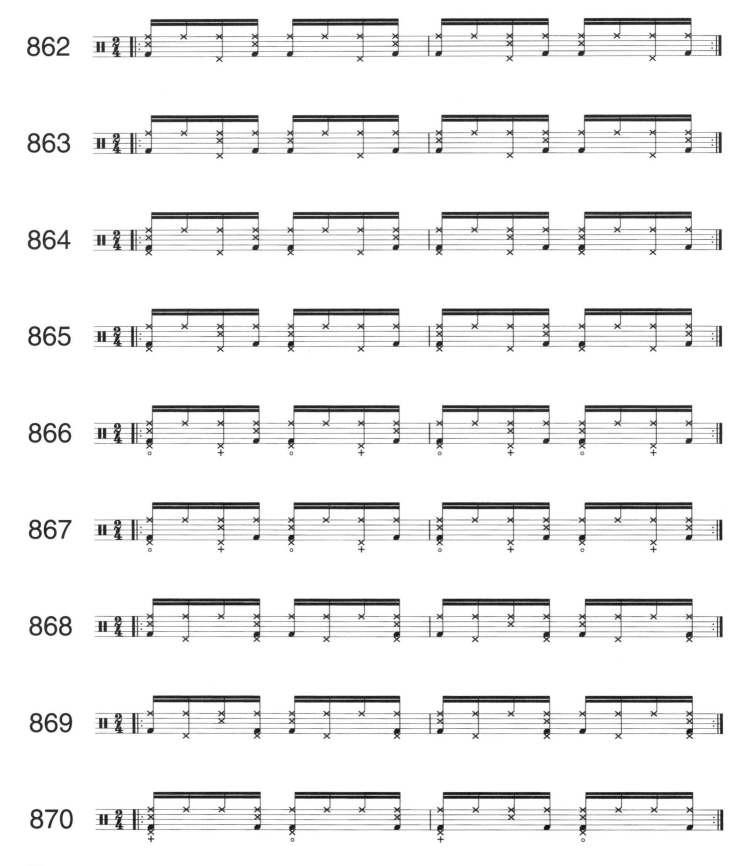

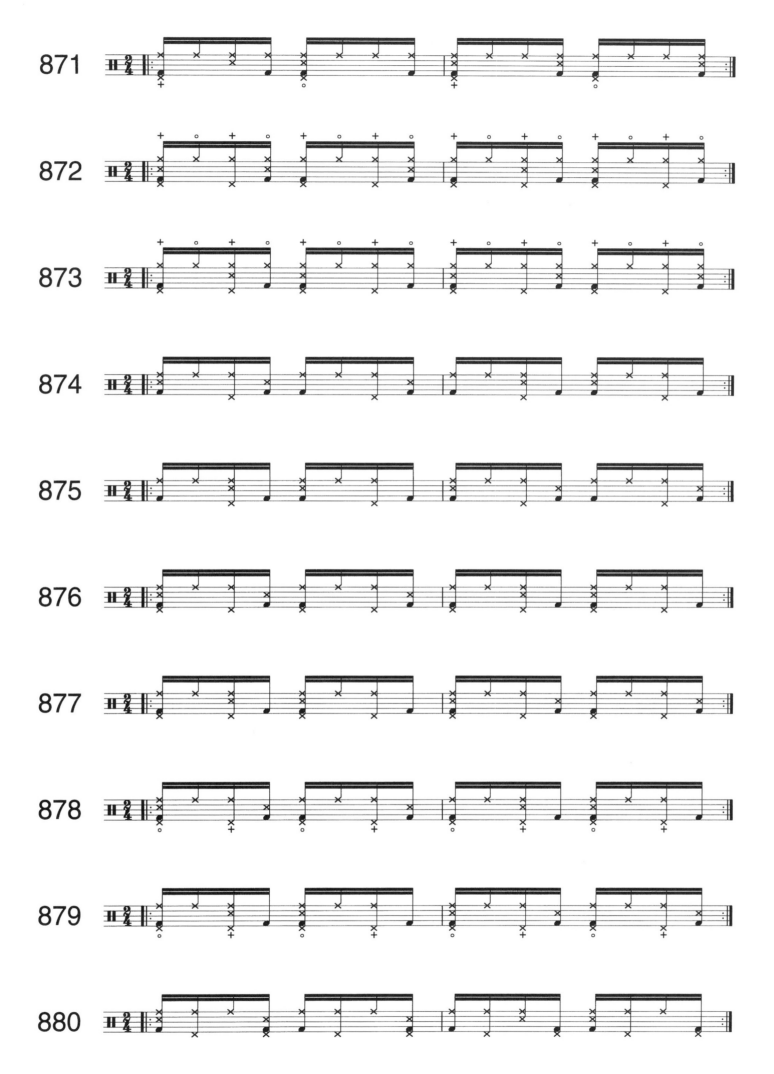

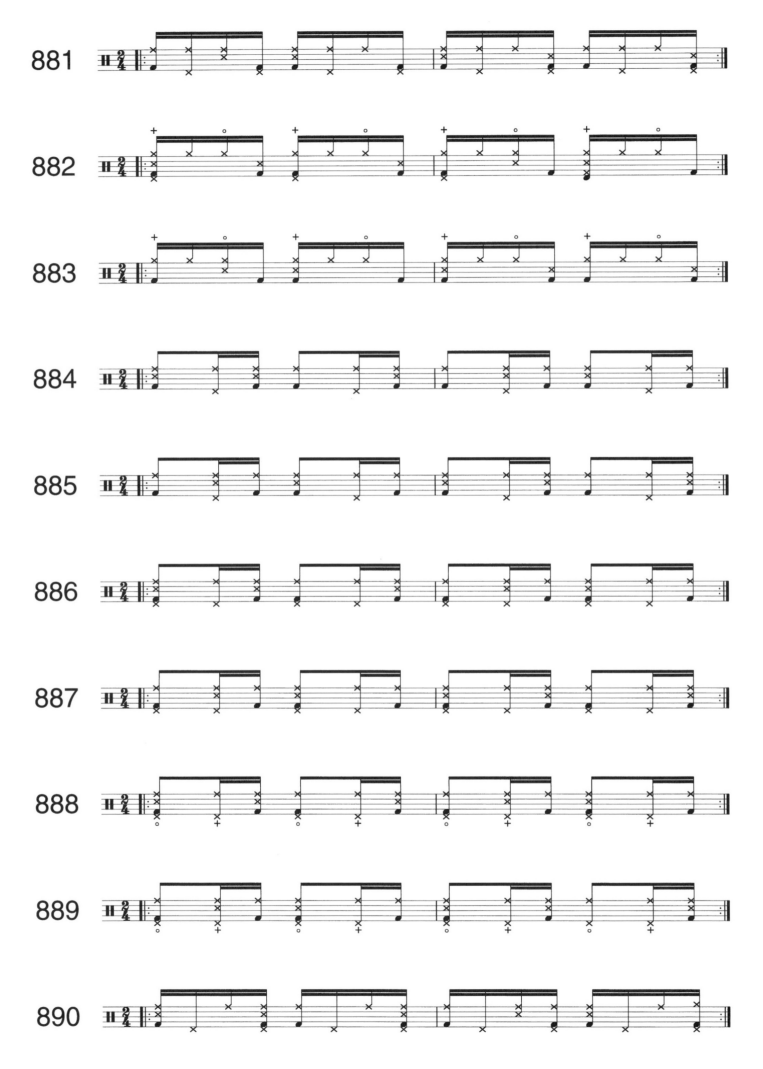

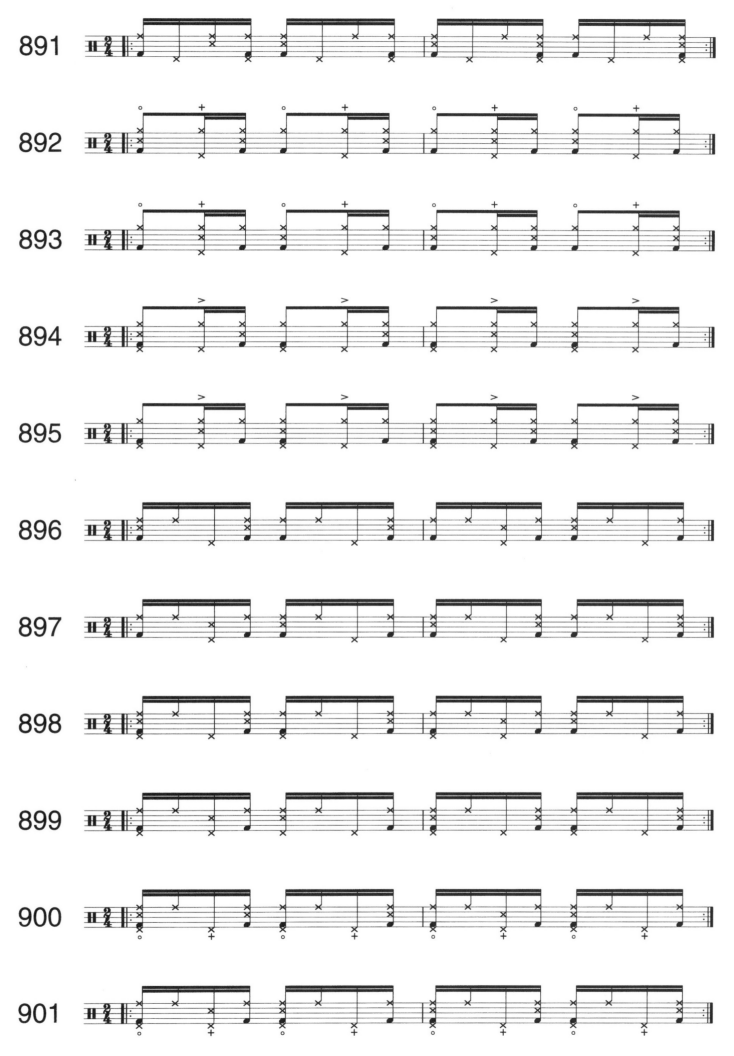

Samba

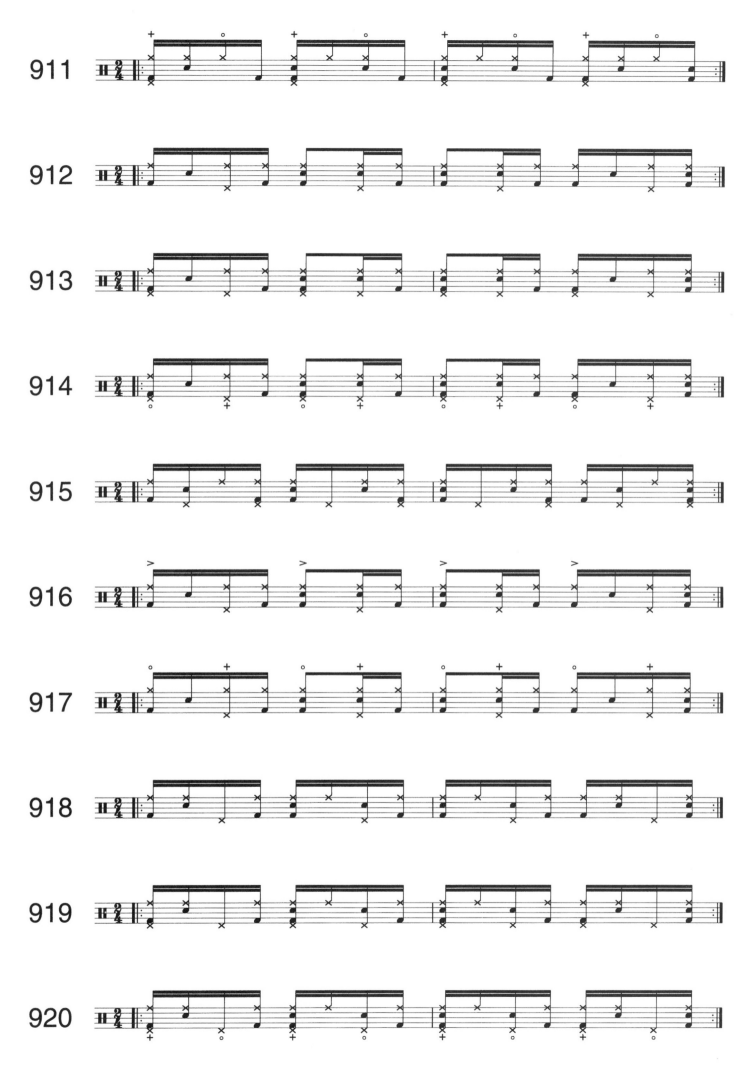

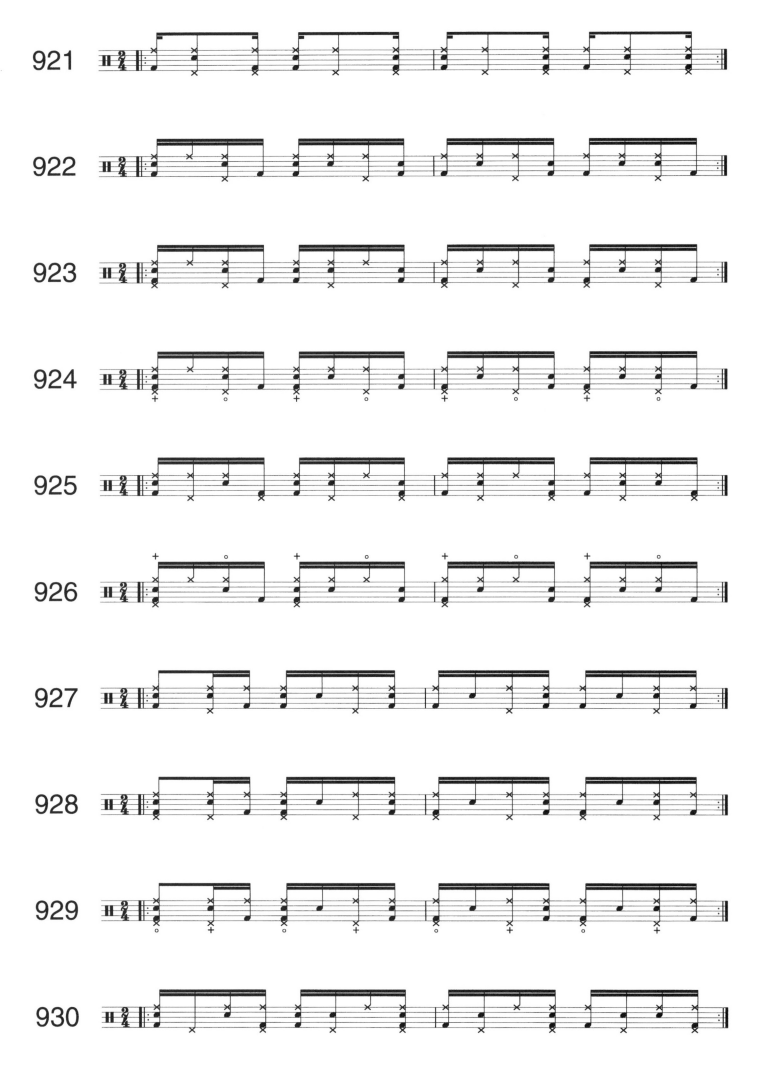

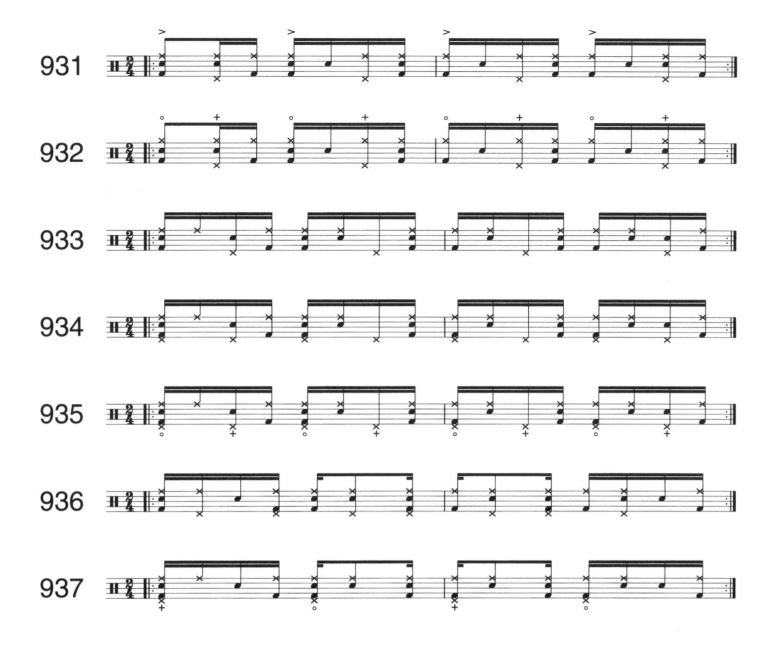

Street Samba

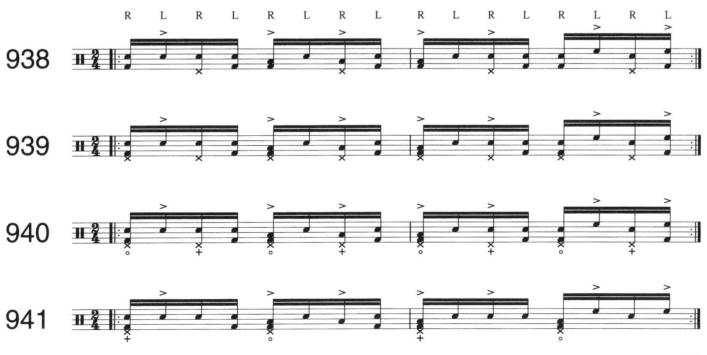

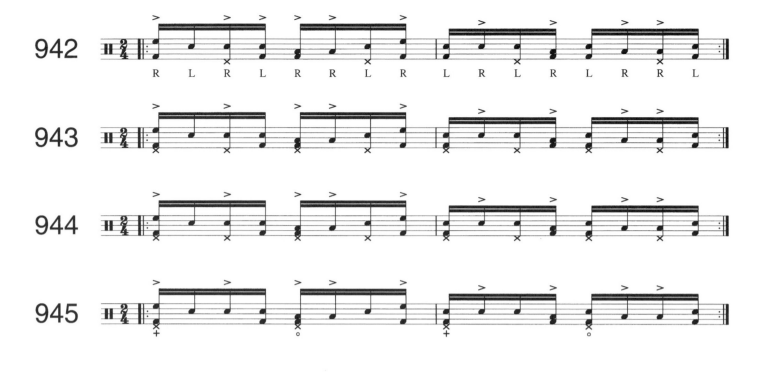

Reggae

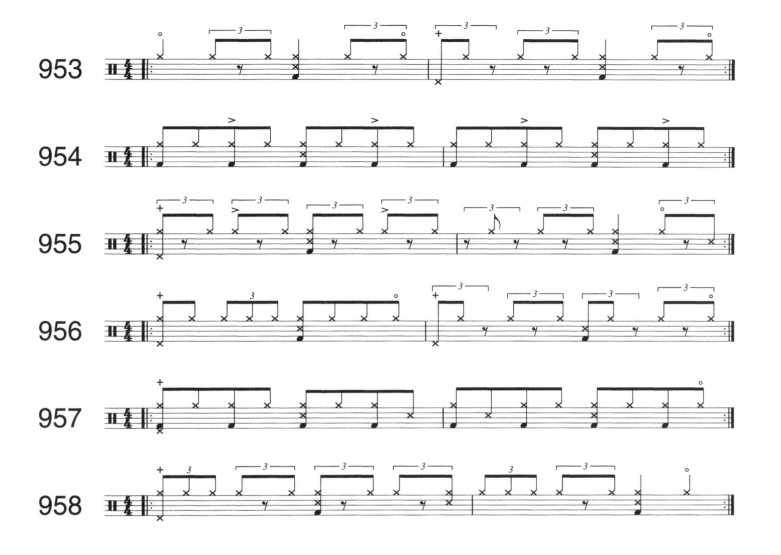

Dance Hall

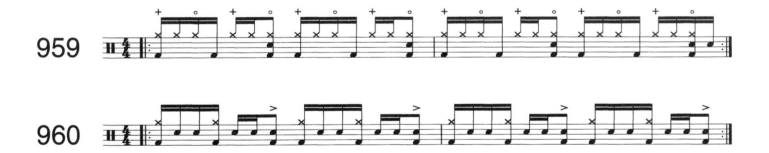

Calypso

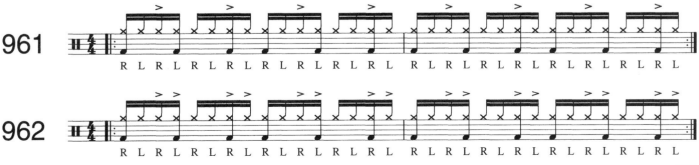

Soca

963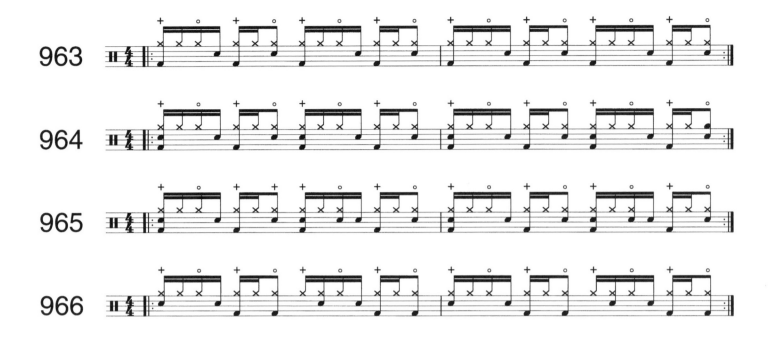

Songo

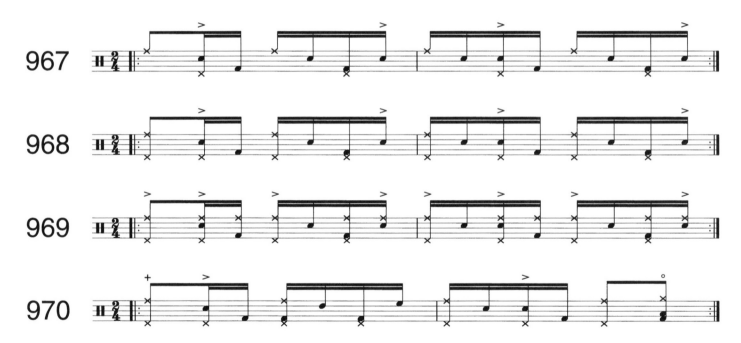

Cascara w/ Son Clave

Cascara w/ Rhumba Clave

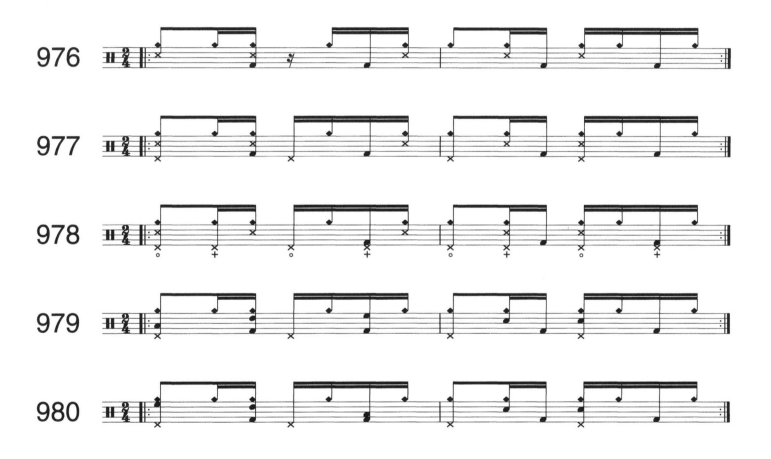

Guaguanco

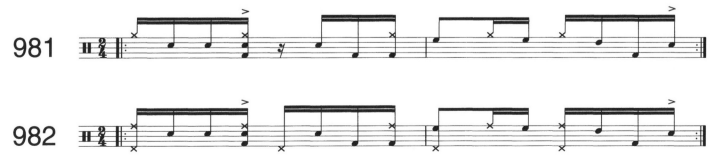

Mozambique

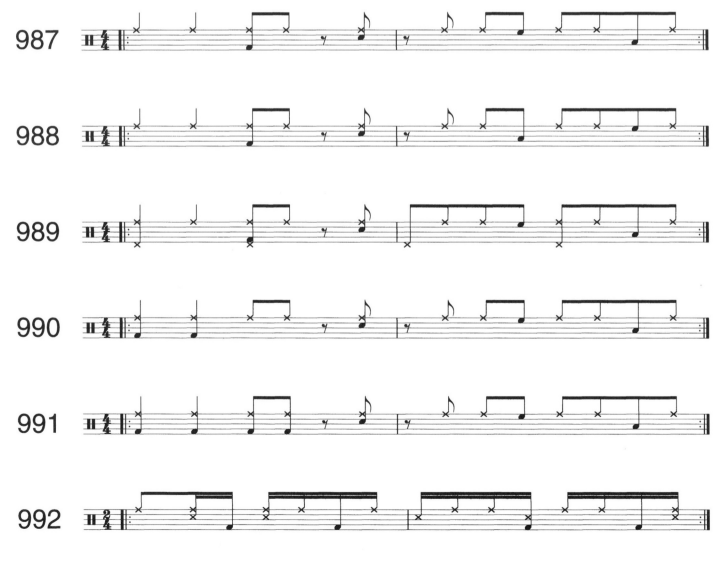

Bembe (Afro-Cuban 6/8)

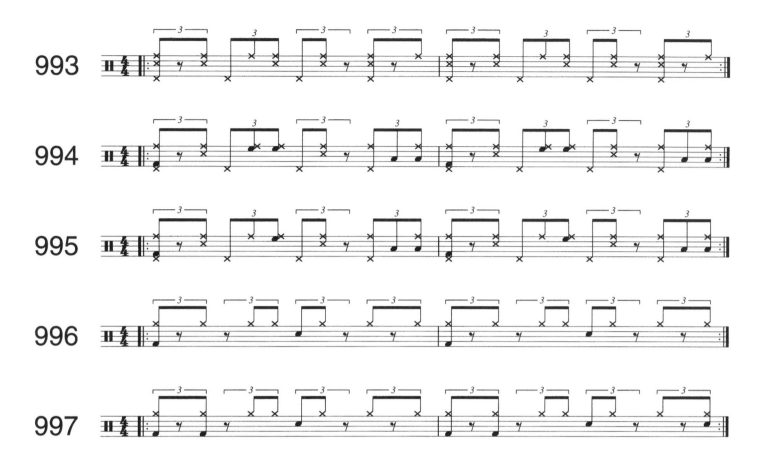

Mambo

Merengue

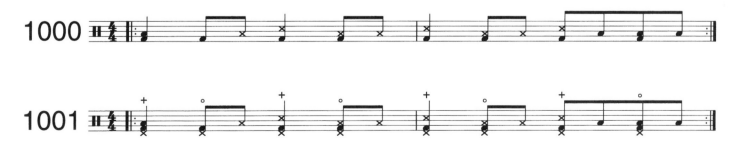

DRUMSET NOTATION
FIVE PIECE SET

Snare

| Snare | Ghost note | Rim shot | Cross stick | Buzz |

Bass & Toms

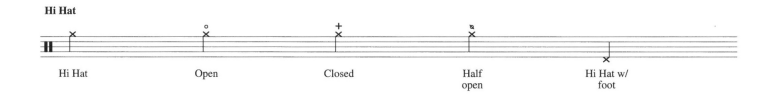

| Bass | Bass 2 | Hi Tom | Middle Tom | Low Tom | Rim of Low Tom |

Hi Hat

| Hi Hat | Open | Closed | Half open | Hi Hat w/ foot |

Cymbals

| Ride | Crash | China | Splash | Cow Bell |